Tales of Old Wiltshire

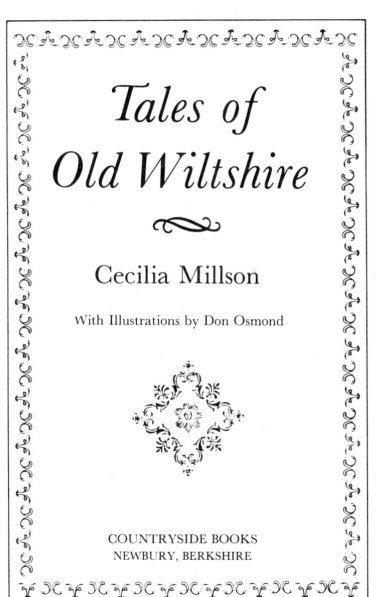

Tales of
Old Wiltshire

Cecilia Millson

With Illustrations by Don Osmond

COUNTRYSIDE BOOKS
NEWBURY, BERKSHIRE

First Published 1982
Cecilia Millson 1982
Reprinted 1987

COUNTRYSIDE BOOKS
3 CATHERINE ROAD
NEWBURY, BERKSHIRE

ISBN 0 905392 12 4

The front cover illustration shows the
original moonrakers, two smugglers from Bishops Cannings,
in their confrontation with the excise men.

Designed by Mon Mohan

Produced through MRM (Print Consultants) Ltd, Reading
Printed in England by J.W. Arrowsmith Ltd., Bristol

To my late brother-in-law
Herbert Williams
who loved his native Wiltshire

Contents

WILSHIRE — The map overleaf is by John Speede and shows
the county as it was in the late sixteenth century.

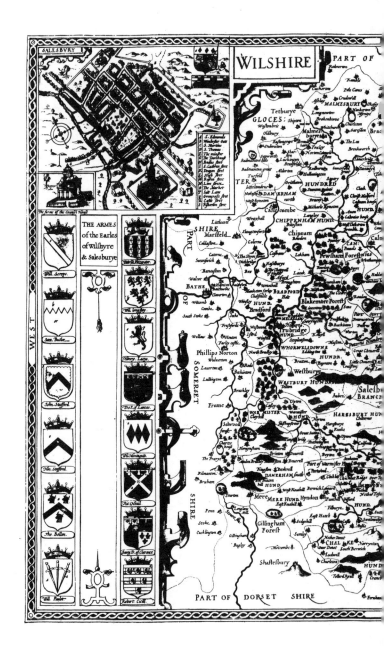

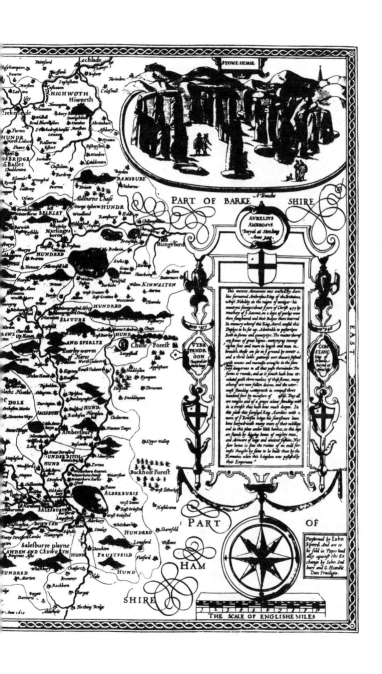

The Flight of an Arrow

OLD Sarum, or to give it the Norman name, Sarisberie, was well suited to become a stronghold of the Norman conquerors. They first built a castle, and then a cathedral on the bleak promontory of Bishopsdown where an iron age fort had once dominated the surrounding countryside.

The first cathedral was started by Bishop Herman in 1078 and completed by his successor, St. Osmond, in 1092. But five days after the consecration a great storm arose and the cathedral was all but destroyed. Only the nave was left standing and this was incorporated in another cathedral built by Bishop Roger between 1125 and 1139.

On his succession King Stephen gave Bishop Roger permission to rebuild the castle in stone, the original one probably being a mainly wooden construction. After the Bishop's death the King took over the strengthening of the castle himself and added a gatehouse, postern tower and sturdier inner bailey walls.

In the years which followed there was continual friction between the governors of the fortress and the bishops at the Cathedral who were annoyed that the keys of the outer gates of the city were held by the governors, thereby making the movements of the ecclesiastical community dependent upon the rules of the garrison.

Eventually a petition was sent to Pope Honorius III for permission to build a new cathedral in the meadows below the hill where the clergy could be more independent. Other reasons were also put forward to substantiate the need for a removal from the hill. There was a shortage of water, and access to the only available supply was dependent not only on the governor's authorisation for its use, but also upon the payment of the price he demanded.

The winds around the hill were almost unbearable and not only damaged the fabric of the cathedral but drowned the voices of those celebrating the divine offices. It was further claimed that the whiteness of the cliffs was causing blindness, that there was only limited accommodation for the clergy, and that the laymen who came to worship in the cathedral were at times intimidated by the castle guards.

A formidable list this, of trials to be endured, and as if to add weight to the arguments, an incident occurred in 1217 which severely tried the patience of Bishop Richard Poore and his flock.

The Dean and clergy had attended a Rogationtide service at St. Martin's Church, Milford, but on their return they found the east gate of the castle barred against them and were forced to spend the night outside the walls. The Bishop was justifiably annoyed when he was told of the incident and lent a sympathetic ear to one of his canons who pleaded, "Let us in the name of God descend to the meads."

It was therefore a great relief when both royal and papal assent was given to the proposed move. The choice of a suitable site for the new building was the next concern and the Bishop and clergy repaired to the battlements of the city to survey the possibilities, and to pray for guidance whilst making their momentous decision.

It is said that at this moment of their deliberations an archer drew his bow and shot an arrow which sped two miles through the air watched by the astounded community. It was an incredible distance and, if the old legend is true, the fantastic flight must surely have been in answer to the Bishop's prayer. It may explain the extraordinary siting of the new cathedral – in a water meadow which was frequently flooded by the waters of the River Avon. It was indeed a strange choice for a building of such gigantic proportions as a cathedral.

The fact that the Bishop owned the manor in which the water meadow was situated was, no doubt, a cause for satisfaction. At least there was no difficulty in persuading the owner to donate the necessary land!

The foundation stones were laid on April 28th 1220. Among those taking part in the ceremony were Bishop Roger Poore, Elias of Dereham the builder, and William Longspee, Earl of Salisbury, and his wife, the Lady Ela. It was as well that the shadow of the future did not fortell that the Earl, a son of Henry II, would be the first person to be buried within the cathedral walls on March 8th 1226.

Thirty eight years after the laying of the foundations the cathedral was finally consecrated. The cloisters were built between 1263 and 1270 and during the next century a great spire was added to a building not designed to carry such a structure. It was four hundred and four feet high and estimated to weigh six thousand five hundred tons – all this on top of a water meadow!

That Salisbury Cathedral now stands so serenely beautiful over seven hundred years later is a tribute to the ability of Elias of Dereham, and the faith of Bishop Poore and his brethren who selected the logically unacceptable site for their new cathedral.

The Drummer Boy

ONE afternoon in June 1786 two men walked towards Salisbury. Gervase Matcham and John Sheppard had been paid off from the man-of-war, Sampson, lying in Plymouth harbour, and had made their way inland. The afternoon was fine and it was good to be ashore after weeks at sea but a clap of thunder warned them that a storm was imminent. They looked at the darkening sky as they felt the first heavy raindrops. Soon they were fighting against the full force of the water and wind.

Matcham suddenly became distraught and his companion glanced anxiously at his agonised face. Suddenly he fell to the ground begging for mercy. Ghosts of the past seemed to swirl around the demented man. He saw a woman, she disappeared, then a large stone emerged before him. Then he ran hither and thither trying to escape from a memory which had haunted him for seven long years. He begged Sheppard to listen to his confession and pleaded that if they survived the storm he should be taken before the magistrates when they reached the next town. The furies of the storm-ridden Plain had cracked his resolve never to tell the story which he then related to John Sheppard.

Seven years before that fateful afternoon Gervase Matcham had enlisted in the army at Huntingdon. Three weeks later he was walking along the turnpike road between Bugden and Alconbury in the company of Jones, a seventeen year old drummer boy. He knew that the lad was carrying some money on behalf of his father the recruiting sergeant, but they were two amiable companions until they passed an inn. Matcham then suggested that they should stop for a drink, but the boy refused and his attitude angered the older man who struck him. The boy fell to the ground and, as he lay there stunned and shocked by the sudden blow, Matcham thought of the money. It would be easy to rob the boy. But as he tried to take it Jones recovered his senses and put up some resistance. In an instant Matcham drew out a knife and slit the boy's throat. Then he took the money and made off towards London.

At first he found employment on the boats on the River Thames but later he signed on for longer voyages and sailed the seas. Always he was haunted by the murdered drummer boy. Now, at last, he had confessed and so the following morning he stood before the mayor of Salisbury.

Matcham retold his story. The mayor, James Easton, was puzzled. The man before him was quite distraught and the ghostly visions were frankly too uncanny to be believed. But Sheppard confirmed the strange behaviour of his companion during the storm and so the story was put into writing. At that point Matcham refused to sign it. The Mayor thought that his mind must be deranged. It seemed probable that he had heard the story of the drummer boy and in a confused state was convinced that he had committed the crime. The mayor ordered that Matcham should be kept in safe custody until inquiries had been made at Huntingdon. John Sheppard was bound over as a witness.

In the meantime the strange story reached the newspapers and as a result two letters were sent to the Mayor from people who had read the report in the Morning Post. One was from Lord Sandwich who remembered the incident and that the body of a drummer boy had been found. The other was from the Huntingdon coroner who was in London when he read the account. He promised to investigate as soon as he returned to his home in Huntingdon. He could not recollect the name of Gervase Matcham but he did recall that the man who had been sought after the murder was described as having a front tooth missing. Matcham's mouth was examined and a tooth was

15

found to be missing. Also, he confessed that he had enlisted in the army under the name of Jarvis as he had recently deserted from a ship and did not want to be traced under his own name.

Suspicion grew that Matcham was indeed a guilty man. His fate was sealed when a letter arrived from Huntingdon confirming the story and stating that in spite of a long search the murderer had never been caught. Gervase Matcham might have remained a free man but a storm intervened, and a long tortured conscience ensured that the murderer of the drummer boy was finally brought to justice.

A Father's Sacrifice

IN the quiet churchyard of St. Mary's, Odstock, there is a gravestone entwined by a pink rambler rose. It marks the resting place of Joshua Scamp, a gipsy who was executed at Fisherton gaol in 1801; but the inscription on his grave clearly shows that he committed no crime:

> In memory of Joshua Scamp
> who died April 1st, 1801
> May his brave deed be remembered
> To his credit here and hereafter.

The story behind these words is a remarkable one of a father's self sacrifice for the sake of his daughter. She had married a worthless, dishonest man, much to her father's shame and dismay. One day the son-in-law stole a horse and, when caught, put the blame on Joshua Scamp who accepted it because of the great love he bore for his child. Horse stealing was punishable by death and the gipsy had no wish to see his daughter widowed and disgraced by her husband's execution. So, the devoted father stood trial and paid the ultimate penalty for a crime that those who knew him well never believed he was guilty of doing.

Scamp's friends persuaded the vicar to bury him in the churchyard, a privilege not usually bestowed upon felons, and a rambler rose was planted by the grave which became a place of annual pilgrimage for his gipsy tribe on the anniversary of his death.

Unfortunately, it was a pilgrimage that often became disorderly for the gipsies also used to frequent the local inn.

17

Eventually one vicar tried to discourage the visits and when the gipsies came they found the door of the church locked against them. They were further enraged when they discovered that the rambler rose had been removed from the graveside. Not only did the angry gipsies then break into the church but they ransacked it and caused damage to the graveyard. The gipsy queen screamed her curses on any who should lock the door in the future, saying that they would die within a year of turning the key. Two people shortly afterwards locked the door, one by accident, one by intent as he had no fear of a gipsy's curse. Both men died within a year. Co-incidence, perhaps, but no one was keen to try again and the key disappeared. It is said to lie in the waters of the River Elbe which flows nearby.

Today, it is obvious to the visitor that care is taken to ensure that the briar rose grows unmolested on the grave of Joshua Scamp who lies honoured and at peace in the country churchyard.

Highway Robbery

THE Kings Arms at Calne still proudly displays the times and routes of the coaches which once called at the inn. "Gloucester, Cheltenham, Birmingham, Liverpool and Manchester — the Eclipse Coach from this office for London every morning at ½ past 8 o'clock except Sundays" and on the second board, "The Hope Coach leaves this office every morning except Sundays for Bath and Bristol where it arrives at 11 o'clock in time for the following coaches: Chepstow, Tinterne, Monmouth and Hereford, also Taunton and Exeter."

A surprisingly frequent service, but the highway through Wiltshire carried the fashionable travellers from London to Bath, and in 1812 properties were demolished and trees cut down to widen the road at Marlborough, enabling the ever increasing traffic to enter that town.

It was with relief that coach drivers reached the safety of the towns where their passengers could disembark to find comfortable inns in which to pass the night, for it was not always safe to be on the roads after daylight had faded. Even the daylight was little protection on lonely roads, and all too often the travellers arrived at the hostelries bemoaning the loss of their money and jewellery to highwaymen who had swooped down on the coaches and robbed their occupants.

On one occasion the Exeter mailcoach was brought to a halt near the Winterslow Hut, seven miles from Salisbury, by the famous Wiltshire highwayman, Thomas Boulter. He made all

the passengers alight and hand over their money before he rode off on his thoroughbred horse.

Boulter always rode the best horseflesh but rarely bought his mounts, a habit which he could well have learned from his father, the miller of Poulshot. Boulter senior was known to be a rogue but was rarely brought to justice. However, in the end it

was horse stealing that was his downfall. He stole a horse at Trowbridge after he had transacted some business in the town in the year 1775.

The animal was the property of a Mr. Hall but the miller cared little who was the rightful owner as he rode away to Andover where he sold his stolen mount for six pounds. As it was worth considerably more than that sum the quick, cheap sale aroused the suspicions of some onlookers and before long Mr. Boulter was arrested and taken to Winchester gaol. He was convicted at the next assizes and condemned to death, but through the intervention of friends the sentence was reduced to one of transportation for fourteen years.

It was about this time that his son took to the road. A year previously he had left his father's mill and made his way to the Isle of Wight where his sister owned a millener's shop. Thomas Boulter started a grocery business in part of the premises but the life was too quiet and the profits too small to satisfy his ambitions and he decided upon a more exciting and lucrative way of life. Using his father's troubles as an excuse to visit their mother he said goodbye to his sister and made his way to Wiltshire, having equipped himself for his new life-style.

Boulter had the good fortune to meet the Salisbury stagecoach near Stockbridge. It proved all too easy to relieve the two passengers of their money and watches so he continued to rob all and sundry with such success that he arrived at Poulshot with forty pounds and seven watches in his pockets.

A farmer returning from market after a successful day was always good game for highway robbery and one who left Salisbury well satisfied with his deals was returning home one evening when he fell into company with a tall, fairhaired young man with easy good manners. Pleased that he had found an amiable companion, not only for the exchange of conversation, but because it was safer to travel in pairs along a lonely road, the farmer had readily agreed to a suggestion that they should ride together. Perhaps the farmer had enjoyed a convivial hour with his friends at a market inn before leaving Salisbury. He was certainly in an expansive mood and confided to his companion that he had sold his cattle for a good price. Then he boasted that he was renowned for his fine beasts and could always command a higher price than many of his fellow farmers.

Thomas Boulter (for it was he) listened with polite interest and said that he only wished he was blessed with such good fortune but, alas, times were hard and he had been forced to take to the road. He was delighted, therefore, to find someone who could help him. With that the highwayman pulled out his pistol and invited the farmer to hand over his money. The farmer was horrified and said that he could only presume his companion was joking, whereupon Boulter dispersed any doubts on the matter by cocking his pistol and pointing it at the farmer's heart. He said that only a gift of money and valuables would enable him to let the farmer continue his journey. The unfortunate man reluctantly produced ninety pounds in notes, and his watch. He seemed very distressed about losing that as it was of sentimental value so the highwayman said that he might keep it as the money was sufficient for his present needs. With this kind action the highwayman wheeled about his horse and rode off leaving the farmer a poorer but wiser man. It would be a long time before he confided in a stranger again.

Boulter's courtesy and unexpected acts of generosity were hallmarks of his methods of robbery. Once he returned a lady's ring because she burst into tears as she handed it to him from her chaise. He said kindly that she could keep it as it was obviously of greater value to her than it would be to him.

His travels took him the length and breadth of England and everywhere he went he robbed until not only the Crown but private individuals offered rewards for his capture.

On 24th December, 1777, a Thomas Fowle of Devizes, who had been robbed by Boulter and James Caldwell, an accomplice, offered five guineas reward for the apprehension of one or both men, while an advertisement in the Salisbury Journal the following month offered thirty guineas for Boulter and ten for his companion. But both men were to enjoy another eight months of freedom before they were finally captured in July 1778. They were brought for trial to Winchester Assizes and, inevitably, the death sentence was passed on both highwaymen.

Boulter's career was short lived compared with that of the 'Golden Farmer' who is reputed to have worked in Wiltshire and the surrounding counties over a period of forty years before he was hanged at Tyburn in 1689.

William Davis was born in North Wales but moved over the border into Gloucestershire at an early age and eventually married a young lady who owned a small property. He prospered as an innkeeper and farmer and became known as the 'Golden Farmer' because he always paid his debts in gold. No-one suspected that most of his wealth came from highway robbery.

Courage, or audacity, made him hold up a coach one day on Salisbury Plain for it was accompanied by postillions and outriders. They appear to have offered no resistance to the highwayman who quickly stepped up to the coach and snatched two rings from the fingers of a surprised lady passenger, but before he could take her watch he was frozen in his tracks by a tirade of abuse to which she subjected him.

The Duchess of Albemarle (whose husband, General Monk, had recently been rewarded with a Dukedom for the part he played in the restoration of Charles II) had acquired her ribald vocabulary in the days of her youth when she was a laundress at the Tower of London. She had been fourteen years of age when she became Mrs. Anne Radford, the wife of a farrier, and supplemented their income by her work. She washed and mended the clothes of George Monk when he was a prisoner in the Tower and on the death of her husband in 1653 she married Monk and shared his adventurous career and rise to fame.

The Duchess was not one to be daunted by a mere highwayman even if her attendants were cowed by his threats. However, before the fate of her watch could be decided another coach appeared on the horizon and the highwayman made good his escape. One can only imagine that the redoubtable duchess replaced her guards by men of greater courage.

Another woman, even if she was misguided, showed no small courage when she decided to become a highwaywoman.

Mary Abraham was a native of Baverstock, a village overlooking the River Nadder. One afternoon in 1779 she rode through Wilton in a suit of man's clothing which she had borrowed from the blacksmith at Quidhampton. He had also procured a pair of pistols for her so she felt well equipped to play her part.

When Mary reached the turnpike road she saw a woman walking in front of her and decided that it was time to start her new career. She galloped up to the unsuspecting lady and drew rein. After engaging her intended victim in conversation for a few minutes she drew her pistol and made the usual demand – money and valuables. Mrs. Thring, for that was the unfortunate victim's name, decided that it would be as well to comply with the highwayman's demands. She had little to offer, two shillings in money and her black silk cloak. The robber pointed to her shoe buckles and the ring on her finger but by this time Mrs. Thring had recovered from the shock and had the good sense to say that her husband was just coming into sight. At that alarming news Mary Abraham galloped off leaving Mrs. Thring to raise the alarm.

Several people rallied to the call for help and were soon in pursuit of the supposed highwayman who by now was a very frightened lady. She was quickly overtaken and the pistol case and bullet mould were found on her person but there was no sign of the pistol. It was later discovered over the hedge where she had thrown it during her flight along the road. The greatest surprise came when her captors realised that she was not only a woman but one they knew well.

The following day Mary Abraham was brought before the Justices of the Peace and on the evidence of Mrs. Thring that she was indeed the robber and the fact that some of the stolen money was still in her pocket, the highwaywoman was taken to Fisherton gaol to await the next assizes. The blacksmith and a weaver from Wilton were also arrested in connection with the escapade but it could not be proved that they knew of the prisoner's intentions so they were set free but bound over to give evidence at the trial. This took place in July and Mary Abraham was found guilty and sentenced to death, but she was soon reprieved. Perhaps the judge felt that a good fright was enough to discourage this very inefficient thief from any further attempts at highway robbery.

William Peare was of very different calibre and successfully robbed the Salisbury mailcoach near St. Thomas's bridge. His method was to fire into the carriage window and having terrified the passengers and startled the coachdriver and horses, he would proceed to relieve the travellers of their valuables.

On one occasion he stopped the Trowbridge coach as it passed through Savernake Forest. The guard, instead of being at his post, was snoozing happily inside the coach and on being disturbed so abruptly he grabbed his blunderbuss and fired through the window. Fortunately for William Peare he fired from the wrong side of the coach, but if it did not harm the highwayman at least it scared him into riding away without any booty.

Like most of his confederates Peare ended his life on the scaffold. After execution at Salisbury his body was taken to a place near Chippenham, where he had once robbed the mail coach. He had been captured at the time of the robbery but had managed to escape to continue his reckless career. His remains were hung in chains as a warning to other highwaymen that they would ultimately be brought to justice and pay for their crimes. However, after two months it was time for Chippenham Fair and a number of his friends were noticed on the fairground. The next day Peare's body was no longer on the gibbet.

The public showed a macabre interest in the hanging of these criminals. At Purton Stoke many thousands gathered in the year 1819 to see the end of Robert Watkins. With his brother, Edward, he had stood trial for the murder of Stephen Rodway, a salt merchant of Cricklade who was returning home from Wootton Bassett on the 7th May, 1819, just as the light was fading. He was waylaid and shot and the two brothers were arrested for the crime but Edward was later acquitted as the only part he had played was to bury the pistol, but there was evidence enough to convict Robert.

The notes stolen from Rodway were marked and his son-inlaw was able to identify two which had been paid to a draper by the guilty man. Another was found at the house where he had lodged while working on the canal at Chichester during which time he had become more than friendly with the landlady's daughter, in spite of being a married man.

Watkins was condemned to be hanged near the scene of his crime on July 30th and so was brought from Fisherton gaol, Salisbury, to the Moor Stones near Purton Stoke.

Two hundred special constables were sworn in to deal with any disturbance as a large crowd was expected and did, in fact, assemble. Fortunately, just as the hanging took place, a violent thunderstorm occurred which effectively dispersed the several thousand onlookers before any trouble arose, but not before parts of the dead man's clothing had been seized as souvenirs. His boots and braces were around long after his body had been buried at Moor Stones which today is known as Watkin's Corner.

Perhaps the strangest of all highwayman stories was told by John Aubrey in the seventeenth century. An Irish gentleman had a strange dream about a relative who lived in Amesbury. In the dream he clearly saw his kinsman attacked and killed by highway robbers. The Irishman was so disturbed that he wrote to his relative and clearly described the two miscreants.

It appears that the recipient placed little value on the contents of the letter for soon afterwards he set off alone across the Downs. Just as the dream had foretold he was attacked and killed. When his body was discovered the letter was found in his pocket and it so exactly described two men who were apprehended that they were convicted and executed for the crime.

Grovely, Grovely, Grovely

MANY commons and woodlands were enclosed during the late eighteenth and early nineteenth centuries. Fortunately, some commoners were able to retain their ancient rights by the courage and determination of men and women who stood firm, and demanded that the privileges which they had enjoyed since time immemorial should continue both in their time and that of their descendents. This is the story of just such a case.

The people of Wishford Magna and Barford St. Martin had the right to take dead wood from Grovely Forest near Wilton. No-one knows when the practice started although it was confirmed as an ancient right in a charter of 1603. The charter also gave the villagers of Wishford Magna the means to 'make merry' – half a fat buck and green boughs with which to decorate their village.

In the nineteenth century the Earl of Pembroke, their lord of the manor, sought to stop the wood gathering as his pheasants were disturbed by the villagers when they picked up their sticks. The menfolk all obeyed the order but Grace Reed of Barford St. Martin was outraged and with three other women, Fanny Pomeroy, Ann Hibberd and Sarah Abraham, she went to gather the sticks as she had done since childhood. The four women were arrested and fined but they refused to pay and so were committed to prison. However, they stayed there just one day for it was proved that they were within their rights to collect the wood and so were immediately released. From that day to this no-one has challenged the wood gatherers and the act of four brave women is now celebrated by an annual dance, on May 29th, in front of Salisbury Cathedral to the cries of "Grovely, Grovely, Grovely, all Grovely". Four ladies carry 'nitches' or bundles of dry sticks into the Cathedral and the ancient charter is read from the High Altar.

And in the village of Wishford Magna the people 'make merry' in festivities which are held as they have been throughout the centuries. A procession marches through the street headed by the schoolchildren who are led by their May Queen, and a celebration lunch takes place in a marquee. A green bough, hung from the church tower, serves as a reminder of the ancient rights and brings blessing on all who are married during the ensuing year.

In very olden times the revels were held on days between Maundy Thursday and Whit Monday but after the restoration of King Charles II in 1660 they were changed to Oak Apple Day, May 29th. This was the King's birthday and the day on which he rode through London in great state to celebrate his return to the throne.

The Wishford Oak Apple Club was formed in 1892 to preserve the rights of the people of Wishford in Grovely Forest. Its members ensure that the merry making continues, as it has done since the mists of time, and that Grace Reed and her companions are remembered with gratitude as the wood from Grovely Forest is carried into Salisbury's beautiful cathedral.

Ansty's Maypole

DANCING and laughter have always gone hand in hand with May Day since earliest times and throughout the centuries merry bands of youngsters have brought Maypoles to their village greens to provide focal points for the day's festivities.

Some tall maypoles stood from year to year, only being renewed when they showed signs of age and the village elders considered them to be dangerous. But an act of Parliament in 1644 dealt a sad blow to these fine upstanding poles for churchwardens and constables were ordered to remove them at once and to see that they were never re-erected. The Puritans regarded maypoles as "a treacherous vanity generally abused to superstition and wickedness". This law was speedily repealed in 1660 when King Charles II returned to the throne of England. Once again the maypoles were erected, crowned with flowers, plaited with ribbons and encircled by dancing feet as the fiddlers happily recalled old Mayday tunes.

Since then the Maypole has been revered or rejected according to the whims of each successive generation. In Ansty the villagers have remained faithful to the Mayday tradition and have kept their maypole standing in the village street. How well it looks, a larch pole, seventy feet in height, standing proudly outside the village inn. The red reflector plates around its base are the only concession to modern traffic requirements.

Ansty is a beautiful village and a perfect setting for an ancient ceremony. The church, manor house and hospice, built by the Knights Hospitallers of the Order of St. John of Jerusalem in the

early thirteenth century, are grouped around the fishpond
which once supplied the members of the Commandery with fish
for their table. Today it is the habitat of stately swans and their
more humble cousins, the farmyard ducks. Both species enhance
the beauty of this tranquil village which throbs with excitement
every Mayday.

The Maypole is garlanded for the occasion with wildflowers
gathered from the woods which surround Ansty. The May
Queen's chair is placed in readiness for the girl chosen to be the
new queen and ribbons are fastened to the pole as the busy
stallholders arrange their wares in front of the Maypole Inn. Hot
sausages sizzle in the pans in readiness for the onlookers who
may be glad of a warm snack on a chilly evening. However, cool
May breezes do nothing to quell the enthusiasm of the crowd as
it waits for the appearance of the little procession. Soon the
queen appears, followed by her attendants, and solemnly she
takes her place in front of the giant pole. The retiring queen
places the floral crown on the head of her successor and another
link is formed in the long chain of Ansty's queens.

As traditional tunes are played the children dance around the
pole and the traffic is brought to a standstill as the dancers swing
out across the road. The ribbons are plaited, unwound, and
replaited in intricate patterns as the schoolteachers watch
anxiously, but all is well; the children have been well trained
and no-one makes a false move. The spontaneous applause tells
the children that they have done well as they trip away leaving
the band to continue the evening's entertainment.

Once in every twenty five years an additional ceremony takes
place for the maypole has to be renewed for safety's sake. Only
twelve hours are allowed for the necessary work to be carried
out. The road has to be closed to all traffic from twelve midnight
to twelve noon. By the observance of this traditional custom
Ansty retains its ancient right to have a maypole in the village
street, a right which has existed from time immemorial although
no-one knows the exact date that the first one was erected. So
determined are the villagers to protect this ancient right that
digging commences as the first pale streaks of light announce
that May morning has dawned. Working in shifts, the men of

this tiny village labour on, asking for no reward but that of keeping their maypole.

The present maypole, given from the Wardour woods by Mr. John Arundel, was erected in 1962. Willing hands completed the work by the appointed hour. Then the tired men were able to relax and stand back to survey their handiwork while their wives and daughters brought well earned refreshment to them. Ansty's new maypole was suitably decorated with flowers, flags, and ribbons, before being blessed by the Vicar. The May Queen was crowned and the usual festivities commenced.

Another era had begun in the life of the village. I wonder if the dancing children paused to think that it would be their children who would be dancing around the next new maypole of Ansty in 1987!

The Flying Monk

DURING the twentieth century man has made incredible progress in the world of flight, but it was as early as the eleventh century that a monk of Malmesbury made his attempt to fly through the air.

It seems strange that it was so many centuries before others emulated his dream and made it a reality. Perhaps the eleventh century monk was inspired by the sculptured angels of the magnificent tympanum above the Abbey doorway, thought to date from the Saxon era; or did he simply envy the birds as they circled the roof tops and then swooped downwards to skim the cool waters of the Avon far below?

Whatever his motive it was not fanciful dreaming alone that made monk Elmer contemplate the exciting possibility of flight; he was renowned for his scientific knowledge. He made himself a strong pair of wings and then waited for favourable weather conditions before making his way to the top of the Abbey tower.

His fellow monks must have watched and prayed fervently as he stood poised for flight on the edge of the parapet. Then came the moment for his courageous leap into space, and with wings outspread Elmer swooped away and flew for a furlong before the law of gravity brought him forcefully to the ground. Miraculously he was not killed but his legs were smashed in the fall.

The frustrated aeronaut was convinced that he had failed because he had neglected to make and wear a tail and he was quite willing to try again with the aid of that appendage. Perhaps it was as well for him that the Abbot forbade any

further attempts. Elmer was already crippled enough and limped for the remainder of his life.

When restoration work was carried out at Malmesbury Abbey in 1928 four windows were placed in the vestry at the end of the south aisle. One depicts Elmer holding his wings in contemplation of his historic flight.

Blackford – the Swindon Backsworder

"**B**LOOD!" – the umpire's call rang out and Blackford of Swindon lowered his cudgel. It was the fourteenth time he had heard the call that day and he was well satisfied. He had come to take part in the backswording contest at Bucklebury, a village in Berkshire, where an annual fair, the Chapel Row revels, was in progress. It was not the only time he played there but this was his greatest performance and would be remembered for many years to come.

Blackford's left arm was freed from his side where it had been strapped in accordance with the rules of the game, and he rubbed his right arm, tired from swinging the cudgel so many times that day. To the cheers of the crowd, and those of his fourteen sore-headed opponents, for he was respected as a fair and sporting player, Blackford stepped forward to receive the lord of the manor's prize, a purse of five guineas.

The champion had travelled far from his native town to play at Bucklebury but he was used to that, for he frequently entered contests in Berkshire and Somerset as well as playing in his own county where his name was a household word.

A three day contest between Wiltshire and Somerset was held at Salisbury Races in 1783. On Wednesday the visiting team stole the honours, a Somerset man called Jupe winning three bouts to take the prize of the day.

On the Thursday Blackford was matched against a notable

35

Somerset man by the name of Stevens but neither backsworder managed to make the blood flow one inch on his opponent's head which was the necessary condition if a hit was to be recorded. Friday was the home team's day for Blackford broke Jupe's head to give Wiltshire victory on the final day of play.

A later contest gave rise to angry scenes as the men from Somerset padded their arms with wads of wool, much to the disgust of the Wiltshire players and their supporters. At the end of the contest Blackford offered to stake twenty guineas of his own money if any Somerset player would meet him in a month's time but, he added, "there must be no padding – let us depend on our own skill." No-one came forward to take up the challenge although the offer was loudly applauded by the onlookers. Stevens of Somerset was playing again at this event and became involved in an argument with the ringside supporters who would have assaulted him but for the intervention of Blackford who gamely defended his opponent.

Public opinion caused the decline of this violent sport in the nineteenth century but while it was in favour it had many adherents and large sums of money changed hands at the ringside as supporters from all ranks of society backed their fancied champions. The backsworders appeared to enjoy the bouts, especially the old gamesters who had survived and won many fights due to their skill with the cudgels. Some unfortunate young players quickly faded from the scene as a result of injuries which could prove serious, even fatal, if the play became excessively rough.

However, an old Berkshire gamester once declared, "Bless you! I be that fond o' thay sticks, I assure you gen'l'men I'd as lief meet a man as is a man for a bout wi' thay sticks as I would – a joint of roast beef."

By that criterion Blackford the Wiltshire champion enjoyed the best of both worlds – he was, by trade, a butcher!

A King Visits Stonehenge

THE famous and the humble have made the pilgrimage to Stonehenge to gaze with awe upon the great stones, to ponder upon their origin, and the method by which they were transported to Salisbury Plain, but it was in October, 1651, that a king of England visited the pre-historic circle, not in royal state but as a fugitive with a price of one thousand guineas on his head.

On September 3rd that year the forces of King Charles II had suffered defeat at the battle of Worcester, a disastrous conclusion to a campaign by which he had hoped to regain the throne of his martyred father. Now the young king was being hunted by the Parliamentarians and it was only the loyalty of a band of faithful followers, and his own courage, which saved him from capture.

Charles spent days, and nights, passing from one hiding place to another, sometimes resting in a lowly cottage or wayside inn, sometimes hiding in secret places in noble houses, and strangest of all, in the oak tree at Boscobel. Having tried without success to find safe passage to the Continent from Bristol, Lyme, and Southampton it was resolved that the Sussex coast should be examined for a likely vessel.

Consequently, on Sunday, October 5th Colonel Robert Phelips of Salisbury rode to Trent in Somerset to the house of Colonel Francis Wyndham where the King was lodged. He had been entrusted to bring Charles into Wiltshire and no one could have been more worthy of the trust. He was not only a most loyal subject but he knew the lanes of his native county.

The following morning the small party left Trent. A cousin of Colonel Wyndham, Julia Conisby, rode behind the King who was dressed in country clothes and wore his hair short, so that he might pass for her serving man. A fourth member of the party was Henry Peters, a servant of the house. Colonel Phelips led his companions through the back lanes where he hoped they would attract little attention until they reached the village of Woodford by the River Avon, a few miles from Salisbury.

The riders halted at Heale House, the home of a certain Mrs. Hyde just as darkness began to fall. She had been asked to give shelter to Colonel Wyndham and his friends by a Dr. Henchman of Salisbury and had readily assented. As she welcomed her visitors she looked at the young man. Where had she seen him before? Her thoughts travelled back to a day in Salisbury when she had seen King Charles I riding at the head of his troops with his young son Charles, Prince of Wales, at his side. Mrs. Hyde was sure she was not mistaken. This was the boy, now grown to manhood, the wearer of an uneasy crown and a dangerous guest to have in one's house. The puzzled hostess showed no sign of recognition but conducted her visitors to the supper table. There were others present, her brother Frederick Hyde, her sister-in-law who like Mistress Hyde herself was a widow, and Dr. Henchman whom the King had summoned to meet him at Woodford.

From the discreet glances made by his hostess from time to time the King knew that he had been recognised but he was not unduly worried. He had intended to tell his benefactress of his identity so that she might realise the danger in giving him shelter. Then it would be for her to choose whether he stayed or not. Charles had no cause to worry. When the good lady showed him to his bedchamber and he spoke of the matter she assured him that he was more than welcome in her house. Furthermore, she had a secret room in which he would be safe. She said that only she and her sister would bring his food so that no suspicions would be roused in the household. Another idea came quickly to her mind, a way to allay the suspicions of inquisitive servants.

She suggested that the King and Colonel Phelips should leave the house the following morning as if their visit had come to an end. Her servants would then be given leave to go to Salisbury Fair so that the house would be empty when the King returned to take his place in the priest hole.

It was an excellent plan, and early the next morning the King and the Colonel took their leave of their hostess and rode off in the direction of Stonehenge, felt to be a safe retreat on the windswept downs. Julia Conisby also left the house attended by Henry Peters to make her way home to Trent. The servants watched the guests depart and learned with delight that they were now free to go to Salisbury to enjoy a day's holiday.

Charles and his companion arrived at their destination where the King confounded the belief that it was impossible to count the ancient stones twice and reach the same conclusion as to their number. As the stones were somewhat disarranged in the seventeenth century it might have been difficult to count them correctly but the King appears to have managed it where others failed, in spite of being preoccupied with more serious matters at the time of his visit.

The two horsemen evaded the curiosity of any passers-by and returned around noon to Woodford where they were met by Dr. Henchman. He accompanied the King back to Heale House while Colonel Phelips rode on to Newton-Tony, leading the King's horse, until he came to the home of a friend, Mr. Jones, where he stayed the night.

Mrs. Hyde, relieved by the safe return of her royal visitor, conducted the King at once to the secret hiding place before the servants returned home from the fair. There he remained for the next few days during which time Colonel Phelips contacted a Colonel Gounter who was well known for his loyalty to the Royalist cause. He managed to arrange a passage for the King on board a ship which was due to sail from Shoreham within the next three days.

The good news was brought to Heale House by Dr. Henchman and at two o'clock the following morning the King left the priest hole and took leave of his hostess for the second time. This time it was genuine and he met Colonel Phelips at a wicket gate near the river. A slight mishap delayed their departure as the horse which Col. Phelips had brought for the King broke its bridle and ran up the river. After some difficulty it was caught and the two horsemen left the sleeping village and made their way into Hampshire. Towards evening they met the King's faithful courtier, Lord Wilmot, and Colonel Gounter on Broad Halfpenny Down, above the village of Hambledon where the Colonel had made arrangements for the party to spend the night at his sister's house before passing on to Sussex.

On October 15th, King Charles embarked for France to spend nine years in exile before returning to England once again, not as a fugitive this time, but as the rightful King, and free to travel where he wished. So, in 1663, he made a progress to the West country accompanied by his Queen, Catherine of Braganza, and his brother, the Duke of York.

The royal party were entertained at Marlborough by Lord Seymour. On hearing that the Wiltshire historian, John Aubrey, considered that the stones of Avebury excelled those of Stonehenge the King expressed a wish to speak with him on the matter and Aubrey was duly summoned to the house.

No doubt the King recalled his own visit to Stonehenge and the way in which he counted the stones as they spoke together. When the journey was resumed the historian accompanied the royal travellers as far as Avebury to show the King the stone circle, and we are told that he showed a considerable interest in it.

Queen Catherine had journeyed on towards Bath and the King and his brother set out to overtake her but their journey was again delayed. On seeing Silbury Hill, Charles commanded that the coach should be stopped. The passengers alighted and walked to the top of what is the largest man-made mound in Europe. The purpose of its origin has never been resolved but as the King stood high above the Wiltshire countryside and gazed over his own fair land, he must have contrasted that day with the one that saw him riding through the morning mist towards Stonehenge to avoid the curiosity of Mrs. Hyde's servants.

The Wages of Sin

"THE wages of sin are death" is a text which is held before the townsfolk of Devizes in no uncertain manner for the locality can boast of three events which emphasise the reality of the adage, and all are commemorated by monuments erected in or near the town.

When Prime Minister Henry Addington presented a market cross to Devizes the Mayor and Corporation thought fit to "avail themselves of the stability of this building to transmit to future times the record of an awful event which occurred in this market place in the year 1753, a salutary warning of improperly invoking divine vengeance or of calling upon the holy name of God to conceal the devices of falsehood and fraud." The misdemeanours of Ruth Pierce are then recorded.

It seems that this countrywoman from Potterne went to Devizes market on the 25th January, 1753, and agreed with three other women to buy a sack of wheat. All undertook to pay their fair share towards the purchase but when the money was counted it was found to be short. One of the women was doubtful of Ruth Pierce's integrity and demanded of her the missing sum but the accused woman declared that she had paid her share and wished that she might drop dead if she had not done so. She repeated the awesome wish and then, to the consternation of the crowd which had gathered at the sound of the quarrel, Ruth Pierce fell dead. When someone dared to

41

touch her body she was found to have the missing money clutched in her hand.

The second warning can be seen on an obelisk in the churchyard of the parish church of St. John the Baptist. It commemorates the death of five young people whose only crime was that of taking out a rowing boat on a Sunday evening.

A newly wed couple, Robert and Susannah Merrit, together with the bride's sister, Eliza Tiley, and their friends Martha Carter and Josiah Derham, went boating on a pond called Drews, near Devizes, on Sunday, June 30th, 1751.

As a cool breeze swept across the pond on that long summer evening the happy scene suddenly changed to one of ghastly tragedy for the boat capsized and the young people were drowned.

Grief engulfed the families and friends of the young bride and groom and their companions. However, the townspeople then raised a subscription to erect a monument, not only to mark the last resting place of the unfortunate five, but "as a solemn monitor to young people to Remember their Creator in the days of their Youth" and for good measure another text was added "Remember the Sabbath Day to keep it Holy."

A more obvious crime gave rise to yet another admonitory inscription, this time on a wayside stone which can still be seen on the road from Devizes to West Lavington.

The stone records the place where Mr. Matthew Deane, a wealthy farmer of Imber, was robbed on the evening of October 21st, 1839, as he returned from the fair at Devizes.

Four highwaymen attacked the lone horseman whom they pulled to the ground. While he was held down the contents of his pockets were taken by the miscreants who then made off with their booty. Mr. Dean pursued them and presumably called others to help him for the robbers were chased continuously as they made their way to the lonely wastes of Salisbury Plain. After three hours one man, Benjamin Coleclough, fell dead on Chitterne Down, two others were captured exhausted that night. The fourth was taken within the next few days.

Perhaps the dead man was more fortunate than his three confederates, Thomas Saunders, George Waters and Richard Harris, for when they stood trial at Devizes quarter sessions they were sentenced to be transported for a period of fifteen years.

One wonders if any of the wretched men lived to return to the scene of their crime and read "that this monument was erected by Public Subscription as a warning to those who presumptuously think to escape the punishment which God has threatened against thieves and robbers."

Beware –
Lion on the Road!

THE village of Winterslow stands high on a hill seven miles from Salisbury. Its famous tavern, The Hut, where the essayist William Hazlitt found peace and contentment, lies in a valley on the main Salisbury to Andover road. Although enlarged and renamed The Pheasant Inn, it still attracts the essayist's devotees and marks the place where an exciting adventure took place on the evening of October 20th, 1816.

On that long remembered night the landlord awaited the arrival of the mail coach as it journeyed froim Exeter to London. The guard had already sounded his horn to give warning that the jolting equipage was near at hand, and there was always the hope that a passenger might alight for a meal when the mail was dropped off at the inn.

As the coachman approached the yard and reined in his horses he noticed what he thought was a calf running alongside his team. Suddenly, to his horror, he realised that it was no calf but a lion and that it was about to attack his offside leader, an ex-racehorse named Pomegranate. The terrified horse lashed out at its attacker but was hampered by the traces. The coach swayed and stopped. There were screams from the passengers. The guard had drawn his blunderbuss when at that moment a menagerie owner appeared shouting at the guard not to shoot his most valuable animal. His mastiff then siezed the lioness by the leg and she turned her attention from the horse to the dog, but she did not kill it for by this time her keepers had arrived. At

44

the sound of their familiar voices she quietened and ran off among the staddlestones on which a nearby granary rested. The coachman and the guard bravely stayed at their posts and an ostler ran from the yard to help with the horses. The passengers made a dash for the safety of the inn.   The keepers took lighted candles and courageously crawled under the granary where they found the lioness lying quietly in the shadows. She was reputed to be a fine animal, five years of age, and normally quite tame. Fortunately she did not resist as the men tied her legs, drew her from her hiding place and loaded her on to a farm wagon. Soon she was safely back in her caravan which was on the roadside en route for Salisbury fair.

The hour of unforgettable terror was over. Poor Pomegranate was replaced by another horse and the coach proceeded on its journey, its occupants, no doubt, fortified by liquid (and dutiable!) refreshment from the inn.

When the coach arrived at Andover two of the passengers lost no time in sending an account of the accident to the magistrates at Salisbury and warned that it was the intention of the menagerie proprietor to exhibit the lioness at the city's fair. He was quickly summoned before the Bench and ordered to secure his dangerous animals properly. The incident itself caused a sensation amongst the public which marvelled at the amazing escape from a savage death on the part of the coach passengers, driver, and guard.

Reports vary as to the fate of Pomegranate. Some state that the menagerie owner bought him, showed him at Salisbury fair where the public gazed with horror on his wounds, and then sold him again; but the Salisbury and Winchester Journal reported that the injured horse was returned to his owner, a Mr. Weeks of Salisbury. As it was considered unlikely that the animal would ever regain its former strength Mr. Weeks received compensation for the injuries inflicted on his valuable horse.

The Spa
of Purton Stoke

CHANCE usually plays a hand in the making of the famous, whether it is a person or a place that is destined for renown. The dice would seem to have been loaded against the spa of Purton Stoke. But if it never attained the status of one of the great watering places the little country spa, or salt hole, has played its part in the treatment and cure of human ailments.

It was certainly very highly regarded by the local residents during the last century and whatever their complaints they went to collect salt water from the spring there. They were distraught when a Dr. Sadler bought the property in the 1850's and proceeded to fill in the well, saying that it overflowed and flooded his land.

The villagers pleaded in vain that it had been used by their ancestors for two hundred years. The doctor scoffed at their claims that cures could be effected by drinking the water and turned them off his property.

As chance would have it, though, the sceptical doctor tried the water himself when he became seriously ill and failed to respond to more orthodox treatment. Wonder of wonders, he was completely cured! He thereupon not only re-opened the well in 1859 but built a pump room around it. The octagonal building may seem small and modest when compared with more famous spas but it served a useful purpose in its heyday by sheltering those who came to buy the water which flowed beneath the boarded floor. A changed Dr. Sadler now welcomed visitors who watched intently as he lifted a trap door to capture and bottle the gurgling water of his medicinal spring. To advertise its true worth he had the following inscription carved over the doorway of the spa, "Sulphated and Bromoiodated Saline Water analysed by Dr. Voelcker 1860".

To the playing of a brass band, people from the surrounding countryside flocked to the formal opening of the Spa, overjoyed that the precious water was available to them once again. Pamphlets were printed singing the praises of the water which was reputed to cure ulcers of the leg, liver and kidney disorders, scalp and stomach complaints, gout, rheumatism and arthritis. Soon the claims reached the pages of medical journals, not only in this country but also in Germany, and Dr. Sadler received requests for samples of the water from sufferers near and far. He sold it locally for one penny per pint and on a commercial scale for thirteen shillings per dozen quarts, carriage paid. It was therefore, at $6^{1}/_{2}$d a pint, definitely more economical to buy at the source!

In 1874 sales reached their peak and £174 19s 0d was realised by the doctor who had once doubted the properties of the water.

Alas, the little spa was destined to fall into decline. Three causes suggest themselves for this state of affairs – a growing disbelief in the curative powers of the water as people became more sophisticated, an increase in the production and sales of patent medicines, and finally perhaps, the proprietor's own personality. His churlish treatment of the villagers in the early years of his ownership of the well does not distinguish him as a man likely to endear himself to his clients. Soon there was little demand for the water either from postal or personal customers.

In 1927 an effort was made to revive interest in the spa. The then owner, a Mr. Neville, toured the countryside in his pony and trap to sell bottles of the water. Obviously he had some success for he continued this enterprise until 1952 by which time he was charging eightpence per bottle and was travelling over a wide area by car.

Today the pump room stands deserted in the meadow but the salt water continues to bubble into the well which is surrounded by now worn and creaking floorboards where the villagers once queued to buy their penny bottles of medicinal water.

The present owners told me that they still get requests for the water, and always take it with them when visiting one or two old friends who remain faithful to the cure which nature has provided in the salt water of their country spa.

All for Love

THE course of true love never runs smoothly — an old proverb which could be well applied to three tales of Wiltshire lovers who had varying degrees of success in their courtships.

A battle of wills was involved in the love story of Anne Beach who incurred her father's displeasure by falling in love with the local curate.

William Beach bought the manor of Keevil from Thomas Lambert in 1681 and no doubt anticipated that his daughter would make a favourable alliance in her new surroundings. His thoughts probably turned towards the highly eligible sons of neighbouring landowners - perhaps one of them would seek his daughter's hand in marriage? A shock awaited the new lord of the manor. His daughter's attention was caught by William Wainhouse, a humble servant of the church.

A modern father would bow to the inevitable but a seventeenth century one was not so compliant and Mr. Beach exerted his authority by locking his refractory daughter in her room for two years! If he wanted her to forget her lover it was a strange place to choose for her imprisonment. Her bedroom was above the porch of the manor house which stands to this day opposite the church. As William Wainhouse walked down the path to participate in the services Anne must have seen him from her window. How could she forget him?

At the end of two years her love burned as strongly as ever and the strong willed girl, who obviously had inherited her father's determination, resisted all attempts to make her conform to her

parent's will. At length her father despaired and issued his ultimatum. Anne could marry the curate and forfeit her inheritance or forgo her love and enjoy the wealth to which she was entitled. She chose to marry the man she loved. Unfortunately this fairy tale does not have a happy ending. Anne's new-found happiness was destined to be shortlived, for she died three months after her marriage.

Our second tale of love tells of a man tormented by hopeless passion. Tucked away in the winding lanes of the Marlborough Downs is the tiny hamlet of Huish. By its church lies a farm, reputed to be once the home of John Reeve, a young farmer, prosperous, good looking, and a bachelor. This handsome man was a great favourite with the local ladies and could have chosen any bride from their midst, but fate decreed that an injured girl should be brought from the Downs to seek the shelter of his farmhouse and this chance arrival changed the course of his life.

John Reeve fell in love with his beautiful guest as she recovered from her accident but she could not return his affection. When she was finally well again she quietly thanked and said farewell to her disconsolate host and returned to her own home. The farmer's brief dream of happiness became a nightmare as he wandered through the lonely farmhouse, and the empty rooms mocked him as he thought of the home he had hoped to share with his enchanting visitor.

Brokenhearted, John Reeve stumbled across the stableyard, went into one of his barns and killed himself, ending a life which had become intolerable to him. He lies buried in the wayside churchyard overlooking the farmhouse where tragedy caught him in its relentless web.

The tale caught the attention of Charles Dickens who was so moved that he wrote about it in his "Household Words" and through the pages of that popular mid-nineteenth century periodical, John Reeve's sad story was read in homes far removed from the small downland village.

Thank goodness our third story has a happier ending! It concerns Olive Sharington whose uncle, William Sharington was granted the house and lands of Lacock Abbey in 1539 when the Abbey was suppressed by order of King Henry VIII.

Olive's father, Henry Sharington, inherited the estates on the death of his brother in 1553 and had the honour of entertaining Queen Elizabeth who graciously knighted her host.

Sir Henry frowned upon his youngest daughter's affection for John Talbot of Salwerp, although the young man was a descendent of Ela, Countess of Salisbury, the founder of Lacock Abbey, and appeared to be an eligible suitor. Olive was forbidden to meet her paramour or have any contact with him. However, she was evidently a most resourceful and courageous young lady.

As she walked on the battlements of her home one fine evening she saw her lover creeping stealthily through the gardens. John hoped that he would see his love and exchange a few words with her from afar. The redoubtable lady, deciding her enforced separation had gone on long enough, had other ideas. She suddenly jumped from the battlements to join her lover far below. The young man stood rooted to the ground in horror as he saw his beloved come sailing through the air towards him. Fortune was with her as the wind caught in her

swirling skirts which opened like a parachute to slow her descent. Unfortunately for John Talbot she landed right on top of him. He was knocked down and lay as one dead from the force of the impact. The distraught girl forgot the secrecy of the assignation, threw caution to the winds and ran for help. Her lover was revived, although not without difficulty, and her brave, rash act brought its reward. Sir Henry was so shaken by his daughter's dangerous undertaking that he gave his consent to the marriage.

Unlike Anne Wainhouse, Olive Talbot enjoyed some years of happiness and gave birth to a son before sadness came into her life. Her husband died in 1581, the same year as her forgiving father. Her son also predeceased her, but her grandson, Sharington Talbot, inherited Lacock Abbey when she died in 1646, long after that memorable leap from the roof of her home.

Old Wardour Castle

THE woodlands which surround old Wardour Castle and the lake by which the ruins stand give the scene a tranquility far removed from the stirring days of the Civil War when Lady Blanche Arundel gallantly defended her home against a Roundhead attack.

Her husband, Lord Arundel, had left the castle earlier at the head of a troop of horse to serve King Charles I, leaving her to care for their property with the help of the household and estate servants. He probably thought that their secluded home would be unmolested by the Parliamentary forces, but in May, 1643, Lord Hungerford brought troops to surround the castle and demand its surrender.

Lady Arundel refused to submit to his demands and prepared to defend her home with the aid of her faithful staff. Although the action was heroic it was impossible for the small band of untrained men to maintain the defence against overwhelming odds. After a week of heavy bombardment the gallant lady reluctantly surrendered on being promised honourable terms by Lord Hungerford. To add to her distress Lady Arundel received the news that her husband had died from wounds at Oxford on May 19th leaving their son, Henry, to succeed to the title and the now forfeited estates.

Lord Hungerford left Wardour Castle in the hands of Edmund Ludlow with instructions to hold it against any Royalist attempts to recapture the position.

The next months found Ludlow uneasily expecting enemy action at any time. The Royalist commander, Lord Hopton, had advanced from the West Country into Wiltshire while the Parliamentarian, Sir William Waller, had suffered defeat at Roundway Down in July. Ludlow knew that he was stationed in the midst of Royalist territory with the nearest Roundhead camp some twenty miles away.

While he waited he restocked the garrison and looked to its defences in readiness for the anticipated siege. As summer turned to autumn he received an unexpected visit from his cousin, Robert Phelips, who supported the King but came to give his kinsman warning that the castle was about to be besieged. Phelips tried to persuade Ludlow to surrender his charge without bloodshed but the Roundhead insisted that he must obey Lord Hungerford's command to hold it for Parliament.

It was in December that the long awaited attack commenced and it was young Lord Arundel who came to retake Wardour with the help of Sir Francis Doddington, a distant relative of Edmund Ludlow. During the following three months the Royalists sent envoys to the castle demanding its surrender but its defenders felt sure that help would come from their Roundhead colleagues and while supplies lasted they were determined to with-hold the siege.

Young Lord Arundel was equally determined to recapture his home. He planted mines in tunnels under the walls and the resulting explosion severely damaged the castle. Eventually, in March, 1644, Ludlow surrendered as he knew that his stand was in vain. No re-inforcements had come to his aid and he was jeopardizing the lives of his men beyond all reasonable limits. Again honourable terms were arranged and it must have given Lord Arundel quiet satisfaction to accept the surrender of the men who, less than a year before, had forced the surrender of the family home from this mother.

The gallant Lady Blanche Arundel died in Winchester on October 28th, 1649, and her body was brought to the Church of St. John the Baptist in Tisbury for burial beside her husband.

The castle, although recaptured by their son's formidable bombardment, was left uninhabitable and gradually deteriorated into the picturesque ruin we see today, while a new Wardour Castle was erected in the eighteenth century to become the family home of their descendents.

Maud Heath's Causeway

ON the outskirts of Bremhill a little stone lady, clutching a basket of eggs, stands on top of a tall monument, overlooking the lovely countryside to which she gave a precious gift over five hundred years ago.

The statue was erected in 1838 by Henry, Marquis of Landsdowne, the Lord of the Manor, and William Bowles, the Vicar of Bremhill, as a tribute to the fifteenth century benefactress, Maud Heath, who was born in the nearby village of Langley Burrell.

Maud Heath was left a widow and in order to support herself she took her country produce to Chippenham market, but the going was difficult for the track along which she had to trudge with her heavy basket was rough and muddy. As she picked her way through the water filled ruts she thought how good it would be to tread on a firm pathway. So, knowing that she would never benefit from her intended gift, she unselfishly saved her money, invested it in land and property, and at her death she left the means to provide a causeway, four miles in length from Wick Hill to Chippenham. It is still in use today.

The statue built to her memory four centuries later stands in a field on top of a hill. By the roadside there is a stone on which is inscribed:

"From this Wick Hill begins the praise
Of Maud Heath's gift to these highways."

The causeway descends to the valley and, as it passes the little church of St. Giles in the village of Kellaways, it begins to rise on sixty four arches to carry the traveller safely above the water meadows and over the River Avon. Opposite the causeway a monument was erected in 1698 to tell the story:

"To the memory of the worthy Maud Heath of Langley Burrell, widow, who in the year of Grace 1474, for the good of travellers did in charity bestow in land and houses about eight pounds a year for ever, to be laid out on the highway and causeway leading from Wick Hill to Chippenham Clift."

A sundial is set on top of the monument and below are the words "Injure me not".

The path wends its way through the donor's native village and on to Chippenham. At the end of the causeway, near the Parish Church, another stone records:

"Hither extendeth Maud Heath's Gift
For where I stand is Chippenham Clift."

As I stood on the causeway one January morning midway betweeen Langley Burrell and East Tytherton I watched workmen clearing the roadside ditch with the aid of modern machinery. The black and squelchy mud had undoubtedly blocked the waterway causing it to overflow and cover the roadway in the recent heavy rain. If that could happen to the twentieth century road surface it was easy to visualise the state of the fifteenth century lane used by Maud Heath as she walked to market. How wet footed she must have been underneath her long bedraggled skirt. The name of this beneficent woman must have been blessed by many travellers as they walked dry shod along her causeway on their way to Chippenham town.

Magic, Mystery and Murder

THE hilltop villages of Tidcombe and Winterslow, although some miles apart, have much in common – prehistoric barrows, Roman roads, windswept farms, and legends of witches; to be precise, one rather special witch in each village.

These witches shared common characteristics. Both delighted in teasing the local farmers and their attendant hounds by turning themselves into hares and leading their pursuers a pretty dance across the fields. Both did it once too often. The sporting hares were eventually shot and crept away, injured, into the gardens of the witches' cottages. Both witches were found dead in their respective homes with bullets lodged near their hearts. But here, I understand, the Winterslow witch did have an advantage. She was shot with a silver bullet. The farmer who fashioned it from a sixpence had sought the advice of the Rector of Tytherley, who assured him that a silver bullet was quite the best way to solve his problem of witch-cum-hare.

The poachers lost a good friend in Lyddie Shears, the witch who succumbed to the superior bullet. In return for baccy and snuff, she would obligingly go into the fields with a flint and steel with which she would strike sparks to mesmerise the hares. They then became easy prey for the poachers. Evidently she was careful to retain her human form at such times so that she could return home safely!

Before her demise Lyddie was well known at markets and

fairs, also at cottage doors, where the wise ones steered clear of her spells by refusing to deal with her. Those who were not so high minded could fall under her evil influence and would soon do her bidding.

At Winterslow, in addition to Lyddie's adventures, the Roman Road was the subject of old men's tales as they sat together at 'The Hut' to enjoy their ale. They talked of the chariot drawn by galloping horses which passed along the ancient route, and the strange lights which twinkled in Hare Warren, although it was agreed that the poachers might know a thing or two about these.

A lady who lives in the village today told me that her grandfather once saw a headless lady on the Roman Road. He was returning from Newton Tony one evening and after stopping for refreshments at The Hut he resumed his journey across the fields. As he walked along the old road about midnight he saw the horrible apparition. Before this incident he would think nothing of walking to London and back but he was so terrified by his nocturnal encounter that he never made a long journey again, and nothing would induce him to walk across the fields after dark, not even to visit his favourite inn.

This old man knew country lore and was his own doctor. If he was unfortunate enough to cut himself he would clap a cobweb on the wound and bind it up for two weeks. When he removed the dressing the wound was healed – not witchcraft this time, just a countryman's brand of penicillin.

More often than not, in days gone-by, events which defied rational explanation were attributed to the spells of local witches. A certain carter was in no doubt at all that his horse was bewitched when he took some wheat to Warminster one market day.

On his journey this carter passed through a turnpike kept by an old woman who was suspected of witchcraft. She asked if he would bring her some coal on his return but he refused, saying that his horse would have load enough without bringing her fuel. He went on his way not heeding the old crone's warning that he would regret this churlishness. Before long his horse stopped and could not be persuaded to move. The carter stood in the roadway, pushed back his battered felt hat and scratched his head as he looked at his stubborn horse. What was the matter with the animal? Then the muttered warning came to his mind. Reluctantly he sent his boy back to the tollgate with the message that the coal would be delivered on the return journey. Soon the lad came running back and as he sprung up on the cart the horse moved forward. The journey to Warminster was accomplished without further mishap, and the horse willingly plodded home with the extra load of coal on the cart.

Animals are notoriously sensitive to abnormal conditions. It is said that it was centuries before cattle would graze where a barbaric murder was committed near Edington.

William Ayscough, Bishop of Salisbury, and secretary and confessor to Henry VI, fell victim to the Irish adventurer, Jack Cade, and his followers, who rebelled against the King and his councillors in 1450. The Bishop, who was accused of spending too much time at Court, was attacked as he travelled in his carriage near Edington. He took refuge in the village church but was dragged from the altar, taken to the hillside, and stoned to death by the mob. Where the Bishop died, the grass grew rank, and the cattle would have none of it.

In the fifteenth century manor house of Littlecote it is a room which is haunted; the result of a horrible murder.

On a stormy night in the year 1575, Mother Barnes, a midwife of Shefford in Berkshire, was roused from her sleep by the urgent knocking of some servants sent by William Darrell of Littlecote. They did not disclose from whence they came but simply told the woman that she would be handsomely rewarded if she would accompany them to "a lady" who was expecting a child that night. The midwife consented but was surprised to learn that she must be blindfolded as she rode behind one of them. She agreed, though, and allowed the scarf to be tied over her eyes. She was taken to a house (which was in fact Littlecote House) where a tall man, dressed in a black velvet gown, quickly admitted her. He locked the door and conducted her to a richly furnished bedroom. There she saw the lady who shortly afterwards gave birth to a fine son.

No clothes had been provided for the baby but Mother Barnes carefully wrapped him in her own apron and carried him into the next room where the man stood waiting for her. He glanced at the child and then horrified the nurse by telling her to throw it into the fire which blazed in the grate. She refused to carry out this appalling order and begged that she might be allowed to keep the unwanted baby. She promised that she would bring him up as her own son, but the man seized the child from her and threw it into the fire.

The distraught midwife stayed to look after the lady until the following evening when she was again blindfolded and taken back to her own village, but before she left her patient's bedroom she clipped away a piece of the counterpane. And it was this evidence upon which William Darrell was eventually charged with the crime; but he managed to escape conviction due, it is thought, to the fact that his cousin, Sir John Popham, was the Attorney General.

However, Wild Darrell, as he became known, did not escape unscathed. Always a reckless rider, he was killed while hunting on October 1st 1589, and, as far as is known, was laid to rest in the Darrell Chapel in the Parish Church at Ramsbury. An uneasy rest it seems, for his ghost is reputed to ride through the park followed by his baying, phantom hounds.

William Darrell's estate passed to the cousin, Sir John Popham, who became Lord Chief Justice of England, and the property remained with the Popham family until 1922 when it was bought by the late Sir Ernest Salter Wills Bart, whose family owns it today.

Over the centuries Littlecote has become a charming and well loved home but even the warmth of a summer's day cannot dispel the cold eerie atmosphere which pervades that room inside where murder was committed so long ago.

Old tales of the supernatural may be discounted by many in this materialistic age but there are still few of us who would care to travel a reputedly haunted lonely path at midnight or sleep in a room where a strange nocturnal apparition has a habit of revisiting the scene of an earthly crime!

Penruddock's Rebellion

O N February 19th 1655, the Earl of Rochester (formerly
Lord Wilmot, who had shared in the adventurous escape
of Charles II after the battle of Worcester) left his refuge on the
Continent in the company of Sir Joseph Wagstaff. The two men
landed at Margate and made their way secretly to London.

The return was fraught with danger as both men had come in
response to a call from certain Royalists who believed that the
time was ripe to further the cause of the King. Others were less
hopeful, and their fears proved well founded for attempted
risings were soon frustrated by Cromwell's well organised
network of spies, whose information enabled the Protector to
quell the insurrections before they became effective.

One most tragic attempt was made in Wiltshire under the
leadership of Colonel John Penruddock of Compton
Chamberlayne and Colonel Grove of Chisenbury.

John Penruddock had already paid dearly for his adherence
to the Stuart cause. He had fought in the Civil War with his
father and two brothers, both of whom were killed. When his
father died in 1648 John inherited the estates but was forced to
pay heavy fines in order to retain them.

Sir Joseph Wagstaff was at the side of the Wiltshire leaders,
having come on from London with the intention of
commanding an army in the West Country, so hopeful were the
Royalists that men would rally to their cause.

They had planned to attack the judges of the assize court which was sitting at Winchester on March 8th, the day appointed for the general uprising, but news was brought to them that a troop of Cavalry had arrived in the city and the plan was abandoned.

They turned their attention to Salisbury where the courts were due to sit four days later. Their aim was to strike at the judges as representatives of the hated Commonwealth regime.

On the night of March 11th groups of horsemen made their way through the forest east of Salisbury to Clarendon Park, once the hunting place of kings and the site of a royal palace. Sixty men gathered in the shadows of the trees. Soon they were joined by forty more led by John Mompesson of Salisbury, and then another eighty from Blandford.

Before dawn the band set off for Salisbury and entered the city. Their numbers were strengthened by prisoners from the gaol as the doors were smashed and the guards overpowered. Mounts were provided for the new recruits from the stables of the inn yards. The party was reformed and rode towards the judges' lodging. Chief Justice Roller and Baron Nicholas were dragged from their beds. Next it was the turn of Dove, the High Sheriff of the County. The judges were forced to hand over their commission. Sir Joseph Wagstaff called for the immediate hanging of the three men but Colonel Penruddock intervened and their lives were spared.

The High Sheriff was ordered to proclaim Charles II as the rightful king but this he refused to do and the proclamation was read by one of the company. It brought little response from the crowd of onlookers who had gathered to see what the disturbance was about. They showed little inclination to take any part in it.

Disappointed and puzzled by the citizens' lack of enthusiasm but undeterred in their resolve, the insurgents rode away taking the High Sheriff as their hostage. They made for Blandford where the Town Crier proved reluctant to pronounce the proclamation so it was Penruddock himself who called upon the people to support King Charles II, the true Protestant religion, the liberty of the subject, and the privilege of Parliament.

Again, the response was disappointing but the leaders pressed on, sending out parties to rally supporters from the villages. The realisation was dawning that they could have been mistaken in thinking that people would fight against Cromwell's well disciplined army, which had in fact already been alerted against possible insurrection in the West Country.

Some of the men soon deserted and made for their homes before it was too late, but the majority continued to follow their commanders who were joined by a Colonel Jones. They passed through Sherbourne and Yeovil on the 13th March where they freed their hostage the High Sheriff who quickly returned to Salisbury. The Royalists still pushed on nourishing the hope that Cornwall, always loyal to the King, would provide some recruits or, if all else failed, would enable them to escape from its rugged coastline.

Their optimism was in vain. Troops were marching from Amesbury, Salisbury, Chichester, Bristol, Gloucester and Somerset while in Devon a newly levied regiment was ready to bar the way of the heroic little army.

Tired by their long march and depressed by failure, Colonel Penruddock and his band reached South Molton but had hardly settled in their quarters for a much needed rest when they were attacked by Captain Unton Croke who commanded sixty men. Although superior in numbers in spite of desertions, the Royalists were taken by surprise and they, and their horses, were exhausted. They made a gallant stand but knew they faced defeat. Sir Joseph Wagstaff managed to escape but his three Colonels fought on until, with only fifty men left at their side, they surrendered and were taken to Exeter gaol.

In spite of a spirited defence against the charge of treason, which John Penruddock said could not apply as Cromwell was no king, and that he and his companions had only fought for the lawful king and, therefore, were no traitors, the brave rebels were found guilty. Penruddock and Jones were sent to London for further questioning but returned to Exeter on April 17th for execution.

Colonel Penruddock had been allowed to take leave of his wife, Arundel, as he passed through Salisbury and wrote her a pathetic farewell letter from Exeter before he went bravely to his beheading in the company of Colonel Grove. His body was taken to Compton Chamberlyne for burial in the church which he had loved since childhood. His wife and seven children were forced to leave the family home as a reprisal for his courageous if mistimed rebellion.

The Wrong Side
of the Law

IN the present sophisticated machine age when robot makes robot and computers provide instant answers to problems which man took years to solve, it is inevitable that men and women become redundant in industry, agriculture, and commerce. A sad reflection on progress, but today the unemployed do receive some financial compensation which, if it fails to satisfy the desire of most men to be occupied, at least keeps them and their families from starvation.

When machinery began to replace forms of manual labour in the late eighteenth and early nineteenth centuries the picture was different and far from pleasant. Wiltshire was badly affected when the introduction of agricultural machinery on farms and mechanical looms in factories reduced the need for manpower. Hundreds found themselves unemployed with no means at all to support their wives and children.

Bands of desperate men began to roam the countryside. They defied harsh penalties and smashed the hated machinery in workshops, barns, and in the market places where it was displayed for sale.

Many, whose families had worked in the woollen mills for generations, were reduced to poverty, and a tragic rebellion against mechanization took place at Trowbridge in 1803. A group of shearmen organized a committee of resistance against the introduction of gig mills and shearing frames in the workshops. Thomas Helliker, a young cloth finisher was persuaded to join the rebels.

The men assembled in the town with blackened faces to conceal their identities and marched on Littleton Mill a few miles from Trowbridge. It was the property of their employer, a Mr. Naish, and they successfully set fire to it. However, the nightwatchman afterwards identified Helliker as the ringleader, and the young man was arrested and taken to Salisbury. Throughout his trial he protested that he was only a follower but refused to name the real leaders of the gang.

Helliker paid dearly for his loyalty to his companions, for he was executed on his nineteenth birthday, March 22nd 1803. He became a martyred hero to the clothworkers of Wiltshire and Somerset who erected a memorial to him in the churchyard of St. James, the Parish Church of Trowbridge. The inscription on his tomb states that, considering his youth, it could be said that he had few equals. Nor was he forgotten by later generations for the clothworkers of Trowbridge restored his memorial in 1876 as they were 'desirous to perpetuate the remembrance of such an heroic act of self sacrifice'. When many old memorials were removed from the churchyard in this century Thomas Helliker's was one of those which was left, and green lawns now surround his resting place. His story is a tragic tale and a reminder of the hardship which change too often brings at the time of its inception, even if the eventual advantages bring rich reward.

To those whose families were hungry, the sheep-covered hills of the Wiltshire Downs must have been a sore temptation – surely just one from the flock would not be missed!

That the vast majority of countrymen resisted such temptation was to their lasting credit, but some fell and paid a severe penalty – death, transportation, or, as an act of leniency on the part of the judges, a long term of imprisonment in the county gaol. Some stole but managed to escape justice by quick witted and ingenious deception.

At Swindon it was a woman who saved her husband from the law. The old workhouse was divided into tenements in the last century and it was well known that stolen sheep found their way into the building, the vast cellars of which provided a cool, convenient, storage place.

On one occasion the officers of the law were certain that they had correctly traced a sheep's carcase to one of the many tenements. The woman of the house appeared unconcerned as they commenced their search. She sat watching the proceedings and encouraged the men to search every nook and cranny saying that she had nothing to hide. At length the officers took their leave, frustrated and empty handed. When the door was safely closed upon them the woman rose from her uncomfortable stool – the large bucket which contained the sheep's carcase. She had carefully covered the receptacle with her skirts and saved her husband from a harsh fate.

But it was not only the poor who resorted to sheep stealing and the crime was the greater when a man such as Farmer Day stooped to rob his fellow sheepfarmers. W.H. Hudson tells the old story in "A Shepherd's Life". Farmer Day sent his sheep to the county's frequent fairs and markets, where the mutual respect and trust between the shepherds led them to leave their flocks unguarded over night. Mr. Day used to pay his drover to steal from other flocks and add the sheep to those in his charge. This went on for some years until the two eventually quarrelled and the drover went to the police.

As a result the farmer was arrested and lodged in Fisherton Gaol in Salisbury. From there he was taken to Devizes to stand trial but on the way he and the two constables who had charge of him stopped for refreshment at the Druid's Head Inn. Farmer Day lost no time in escaping from his captors and made off on a fast horse, never to be seen in the district again.

It is to be hoped that the enforced exile from his favourite haunts, and the exposure of his duplicity, brought some measure of punishment to the farmer whose guilt could never be justified by poverty or hardship.

Country Pastimes

Shrove Tuesday, Shrove Tuesday,
When Jack went to plough
His mother made pancakes,
She didn't know how,
She tossed them, she turned them,
She made them so black,
With soot from the chimney,
She poisoned poor Jack.

A Shrove Tuesday rhyme known to many country children in Wiltshire and neighbouring counties with variations in some of the lines and a change from soot to pepper for the "poison" administered to poor Jack. However, children cared little for the correct words of the jingle as they were freed from school by the clanging of the pancake bell and ran off to enjoy a day's holiday.

When they finished work, the older boys and girls joined the schoolchildren at Bradford-on-Avon, Warminster, and Hill Deverill, to dance through the streets Threading the Needle. The front couple made an arch under which the procession passed and at last, after many repetitions of this mode of progress, the dancers arrived at their respective parish churches in readiness for the annual ceremony of Clipping the Church. The children passed through the churchyard gate, held open for them by the verger, and then encircled the church three times, holding hands and singing the Shrove Tuesday rhyme. Afterwards they would return to their homes to enjoy a supper of pancakes before starting the Lenten fast.

A variation of Threading the Needle was celebrated at Marlborough up to a hundred years ago. Jacky John's Fair was held in May and people gathered in Poulton Meadows by the River Og to join hands and dance through the town. They would go to the Town Hall, circle round the pillars, and then return to the meadows singing as they danced: "The tailor's blind and he can't see, so we will thread the needle". They ended the ceremony by throwing articles into the river before enjoying themselves at the fair. It was this tribute to the river which has given rise to the belief that the custom was in some way related to the worship of a river god, and therefore dated from the pre-Christian era.

A Palm Sunday meeting used to take place on the top of Silbury Hill, the pre-historic mound six miles west of Marlborough, when the people of Avebury and district climbed up the steep hillside with their cakes, figs, sugar, and water drawn from the swallowhead springs of the River Kennet, to enjoy an evening picnic; another probable transition from a pagan to a Christian festival which continued until a century ago.

The playing of games in churchyards has been long discouraged, but the church towers of Baverstock and Clyffe Pypard were once used as backgrounds for games of Fives, a ball game in which three fives or fifteen is counted.

Churchwardens' pipes provided the necessary material for a game of Baccies at Potterne. The stems were broken into three inch lengths and placed a few inches from a wall. Then a large marble was bowled towards the upstanding targets and the boy who could knock down the most stems won the game. The thick end which had adjoined the bowl of the pipe was called the Granger Baccie and carried a special score.

This game gave the boys good practice for the more adult game of skittles. As three of the six inns in the village had skittle alleys it was a popular pastime, and was played also at the Potterne Feast which was held on the first Sunday after the 19th September. Unfortunately, like many other country fairs, this fell into disrepute towards the end of the last century and the Vicar, Archdeacon Buchanan, and his successors, applied themselves to the work of making the feast more respectable so that it could be enjoyed by all their parishioners.

The inhabitants of some Wiltshire villages took it upon themselves to improve the morals of their neighbours by the old custom of Wooset Hunting.

If infidelity was suspected in a marriage partnership the young men of the village collected old frying pans, saucepans, kettles, cracked sheep bells, in fact anything which was capable of increasing the raucous noise of their 'rough band'.

During the evening a call would be sounded on a sheep's horn. That was the signal for the bandsmen to fall in on parade. At the centre of the procession one man would carry a horse's skull attached to a long pole. By the skilful manipulation of a piece of string the jaws would be made to clack whenever there was a lull in the strident music.

All in all, it was a formidable sound and one which left no doubt as to the identity of the guilty party as the band would play outside the unfortunate person's house for three nights in succession. Then the bandsmen would desist for three nights, only to resume their labours again for another three evenings, followed by three quiet ones before gathering for a final three performances. Apparently, this timing kept the players within the law. It also gave the weary neighbours of the guilty party a chance to sleep and gather strength for the next onslaught, at the same time keeping the unfaithful spouse in a state of terror as he, or she, waited for the noise by night, and faced the ridicule and wrath of the neighbours the following day.

A quieter and healthier sport was that of truffle hunting, when edible underground fungi were the quarry of the hunters and their highly trained dogs.

In the village of Winterslow lived a family of noted truffle hunters named Collins, who kept the tradition going from one generation to another, the last hunter dying in the middle of this century. They bred and trained their own dogs which were descended from poodles brought over by an eighteenth century Spaniard. He lodged the dogs with a country couple near Stonehenge so that they were ready when he came over to England for the sport.

After the dogs had sniffed out the truffles where they lay under the soil, the hunters would put down a long spike to dig out the dark coloured fungi which have no visible root. Truffles vary in size but particularly fine ones were found on the Longford estate of the Earl of Radnor, and during the last century Eli Collins was given permission to go there at any time for the sport. One of the largest ever found weighed over one pound and was presented to one of the hunting party, the Duke of Clarence, who promised that it would be given to his grandmother, Queen Victoria. In return Mr. Collins was given a photograph of the Queen and a golden sovereign.

As well as truffle hunters Winterslow, in common with other Wiltshire villages, had its own group of mummers. Some mummers are still active today and they present a medieval form of drama as a Christmas or Easter entertainment. To the principal characters of St. George, or King George, the Turkish Knight and the Doctor with his Oppliss Poppliss Drops, are sometimes added traditional and heroic characters, such as Father Christmas, Robin Hood, and Lord Nelson, whose death scene is included in the text of the Quidhampton mummers' play.

Whatever variations occur in the spoken lines, which have been handed down by word of mouth over the centuries, the mummers can be sure of a welcome whenever they appear in the traditional costumes with their multicoloured streamers and tall head-dresses – the origin of which, like the plays themselves, stems from the distant past.

A country dance adds to the enjoyment of any festivity and in the old days a man who could scrape a tune from a fiddle was always in demand, either in his own village or at a neighbouring fair or feast. His repertoire did not have to be extensive; the dancers did not complain and were quite content to hear their favourite tunes played again and again. Sometimes the fiddler would be accompanied by his man of business who collected the pennies from the dancers as they took to the floor on a penny per dance per person basis.

The dancing usually took place on the village green during daylight hours but as the evening shadows fell the party would be transferred to a large barn or the inn. With beer at $1\frac{1}{2}$d per quart to refresh both the dancers and the musician the pace became faster, and the company merrier, as the evening progressed until at last the revellers were exhausted and a halt was called to the dance.

Then, with lanterns to light the way, the more fortunate returned home by pony and traps, or wagonettes, while others trudged on their aching feet which had been beguiled into dancing too long by the fiddler's rhythmic tunes.

Smuggler's Tales

IT is surprising to find tales of smuggling in Wiltshire, an inland county with no convenient creeks or deserted beaches for the unloading of wine, spirits, tea, tobacco, lace and silk, all of which carried heavy duty if brought lawfully from the continent.

However, if Wiltshire lacks vital sea links, the forests of Hampshire adjoin those of Wiltshire and these provided excellent cover for the strings of pack horses which brought the contraband over the county border. Convenient depots housed the smuggled goods until they could be distributed to eager and discreet customers.

The customs officers were ever watchful but they had a difficult task for it was a fact that some men in high positions were hand in glove with the smugglers and were quite willing to turn a blind eye providing that a keg of brandy or rum was left in their stables by the riders who passed in the night.

In 1783 the officers were delighted when six hundred pounds of tea were discovered in the house of Mr. Sheppard of Cheriton. The householder was promptly taken before the magistrates and fined one hundred and fifty pounds. Although a hefty sum of money in the eighteenth century the fine was paid the same day. No doubt Mr. Sheppard was only too pleased that he had escaped with a fine instead of being committed to the county gaol.

The tea was confiscated and taken to the house of the Customs Supervisor at Devizes. The officer was warned that an attempt might be made by the smugglers to recapture the contraband

but he laughed at the idea, much to his later discomfort. That evening a group of armed men rode into the town, attacked the supervisor's house, and carried off the tea in triumph.

In "A Shepherd's Life" a story is told by W.H. Hudson of a well respected carrier and small farmer of Hindon whose duplicity came as a surprise to his neighbours. Consignments of rum and brandy were delivered to him by night and carefully hidden in his farmyard manure heap or under a pit in the pigsty. The carrier's wife and their son, who had been blind since childhood but was capable of driving a horse, would set out on their way to Bath to deliver the legitimate parcels which provided good cover for their more lucrative illegal trading. If they met customs officers along the road no suspicions were aroused. The pair were well known and after an exchange of greetings their cart trundled on its way. They might never have been caught but for one of those simple mistakes which frequently bring the most hardened criminals to justice. They left a jar of brandy at the wrong address. The householder was an honest man and made inquiries amongst his neighbours to find the rightful owner. Apparently he did not realise that he was holding smuggled spirits. No one claimed the jar but his painstaking inquiries came to the notice of the customs officers who quietly relieved him of the brandy and then waited for the next journey of the carrier's cart.

Sure enough, it contained contraband and mother and son were arrested and taken before the magistrates. The son was released on account of his blindness but he had a most uncomfortable journey home. The horse and cart were confiscated as well as the parcels, and the blind youth was left to make his own way to Hindon. It is to be hoped that some whom he had served with illicit brandy helped him on his way.

But undoubtedly the most famous smuggling story of Wiltshire relates to the wily moonrakers of Bishops Cannings who completely fooled two excise officers one moonlit night. The excisemen came upon the smugglers in the act of retrieving some kegs of brandy from a pond where they had been dumped for safety earlier in the day.

As the men skimmed the water with their hayrakes the officers stopped to ask what they were doing, only to be told by the men that they were after 'thic gurt yaller cheese'. The officers pondered a moment and then laughed derisively as they spotted the moon's reflection on the water. They rode off pitying the poor halfwits who were trying so hard to pull it from the pond. As soon as the officers were safely out of sight the real booty was raked to the surface, and it was the smugglers who burst out laughing.

Lawbreakers they were, but those smugglers have endeared themselves to all Wiltshiremen, who have proudly adopted the title of 'Moonrakers' as their very own, and the story has raised many a laugh far beyond the moonraker's home county.

The Bellows Auction

THE Bell Inn at Purton Stoke, with its oak beams and high settles, once provided the right setting for an auction in which the inn bellows played a major part, and the pasture land for which the bids were made is still part of a charity which has a long and interesting history.

The Forest of Braydon, which long ago surrounded the hamlet, was a hunting ground of the Norman kings. The whole area was governed by severe forest laws under which deer and other wild animals were protected for the kings' own sport.

During the reigns of King Henry II and King John the forest was greatly extended by encroachment on neighbouring lands which then became subject to these laws, much to the disgust of the landowners. In 1217, Henry III was forced to draw up a Charter of the Forest after which the boundaries were recorded, the laws clearly defined, and certain waste lands endowed with common rights so that the villagers could graze their cattle and collect dead wood within such areas.

Throughout the next centuries minor offences such as the poaching of small game and the infringement of common rights were heard before the local courts, the Swanimotes, and major poaching offences and boundary disputes were taken to the "Forest Eyre".

In 1627, Charles I set up a commission to end the charter and this was finally achieved in 1630. Braydon was disafforested, crown land was leased, freeholders and tenants whose land was within the forest boundaries of 1300 were compensated by grants of land. Lastly, in 1631, the poor of Purton Stoke were

78

given twenty five acres of pasture land to compensate them for their loss of common rights within the old forest area.

During the next one hundred years disputes arose because the original twenty-three householders and their descendents, some of whom lived in the adjoining village of Purton, refused to allow others to benefit from the charity.

The matter was resolved by the Court of the Exchequer in 1735 when it was established that the land was for the sole use of the inhabitants of Purton Stoke who were entitled to nominate fifteen trustess to lease the land and manage the charity. When the number fell as low as seven the villagers were allowed to name others to bring the number up to fifteen again. These trustees decided soon after this to lease the twenty five acres of land, which are in Cricklade, by means of a bellows auction. During a bellows auction there is no shouting of bids. Instead a large bellows is passed around a circle of bidders with a piece of chalk. Bids are written on the bellows as it goes round. The item at auction is sold to the highest recorded bidder after the bellows has travelled three full rounds without a further bid being added.

One can imagine the landlord of the inn, with bellows in hand, calling the interested parties to order as they sat on the oak settles, with well filled tankards, waiting for the business to commence. The previous year's tenant would be asked if he wished to make the first bid to rent the land for the ensuing year, after which the bellows and chalk would be passed round the company for the recording of further offers. When it was thought that the limit had been reached the bellows still had to make three clear rounds before the deal was finalised; time enough for a hesitant bidder to change his mind and quickly add another figure as the bellows passed through his hands.

Excitement mounted during the third round — would the bellows reach the landlord without further markings, or would a last minute bid be added and so prolong the auction by at least another three rounds?

This method of auctioning was carried out for over a hundred years according to Mrs. Richardson, who wrote the history of the village in 1917. Nowadays tenders are invited for the land which is let every year from May 1st to November 15th, but if the old auction ifself has passed into the pages of history, the distribution of the charity still takes place at the Bell Inn.

As for many years past, five trustees are now appointed by the Parish Council and these are re-elected every three years. In addition, four co-opted trustees are appointed for life by the Charity Commissioners.

The January meeting is held at the Inn on the first Thursday after Epiphany (January 6th) when the trustees assemble for tea at 5.30 p.m. After tea it is decided how the money realised by the current year's rent should be allocated to those who are entitled to receive the charity.

In 1765, the first year the present system of distribution was adopted, the sum of thirty pounds nine shillings was divided between sixteen households. In 1981 the sum of nine hundred and thirty nine pounds was shared between twenty eight recipients in amounts which ranged from fifty pounds each for old age pensioners, widows, and widowers, to twelve pounds each for those who received the charity for the first time. Newcomers always receive less but once admitted their names remain on the roll for life.

During the deliberations of the trustees the beneficiaries gather together in the genial surroundings of the inn bar. At eight o'clock they are formerly welcomed by the Chairman of the Trust. Then the secretary, to whom I am indebted for information regarding the charity, calls out the names and the amounts awarded. The money is spread round a large table and as each recipient's name is repeated, loudly and clearly, he or she comes forward to receive the ancient charity.

In this way the revenue from the pasture land, which, incidentally, was increased to twenty nine acres during the last war, continues to help the descendants of those who lost their very precious common rights three hundred and fifty years ago.

The Lost Mosaic

WILLIAM George, the steward of Littlecote Park in the early eighteenth century, was a keen amateur archaeologist. He had taken part in the nearby excavations at Knighton, and at Rudge, near Froxfield, where he had discovered a Roman pavement in 1725, but when a large mosaic was unearthed at Littlecote towards the end of 1727 he was obviously quite overwhelmed by the sight of this unexpected treasure on his employer's land. The discovery appears to have come about by chance, probably when trees were planted in the garden of the hunting lodge. Unfortunately the steward's enthusiasm was not shared by the then owner of Littlecote, Edward Popham. His only concern was for his privacy, and he made it clear that he did not want archaeologists trampling over his land.

Fortunately, Mr. Popham allowed William George to uncover the mosaic during the winter of 1727/28 and the steward wrote to Lord Hertford, the President of the Society of Antiquaries of London, telling him about his most recent discovery in Wiltshire. It is now thought that it was Lord Hertford, and not Mr. Popham, who then sent the artist George Vertue to make his own detailed drawings from which were transcribed the very fine coloured engraving which is in the Ashmolean Library at Oxford.

Mr. George also made drawings of the mosaic before Edward Popham ordered it to be buried again. Popham then announced that it was totally destroyed and, just to ensure that it would be extremely difficult to locate again, he gave its position as being a

quarter of a mile from its true site and added that it was covered by six feet of earth. Trees were planted at either end of the excavation, presumably to disguise where the digging had taken place. How Edward Popham hated that mosaic!

Soon afterwards William George died, and one imagines he was quite broken hearted that his beautiful mosaic was seemingly lost for ever. Fortunately, his widow sought consolation in her needlework. Mrs. George embroidered a panel depicting the mosaic, which she designed from her husband's drawings. This embroidery hangs in Littlecote House to this day. Successive owners have treasured her handiwork and regretted that the original subject matter was lost through the obstinacy and carelessness of a past owner of the estate.

The Wiltshire antiquarian, Sir Richard Colt-Hoare

expressed his own regret when he wrote of the mosaic in his noted work 'Ancient Wiltshire, Volume II' which was published in 1826. General Popham, who owned Littlecote at that time, allowed Sir Richard to reproduce illustrations of the mosaic from the copper plates and to use these in his book so that his readers could see the details of the design. These had never before been published. After praising the obvious beauty and value of the pavement, Sir Richard added "but, alas, the site only remains on which it formerly existed, which is in a low piece of ground near a river, in the park of the Popham family at Littlecote. I have never heard the cause of its having been taken up, for I should conceive its situation would have guarded it against the dilapidation of the common people." An obituary for a mosaic, or so it was thought, but strange things happen and it is rather pleasing to know that the often maligned rabbits played their small part in the rediscovery of the ancient treasure.

In 1976 a survey was taken of the park which is now in the ownership of Mr. David Seton Wills. A medieval village was known to have existed thereabouts and this was the foremost subject of the survey although the presence of a Roman villa or two in this area a possibility. There was little or no thought given to the chances of rediscovering William George's mosaic.

However, Mr. Bryn Walters, the archaeologist in charge of the project, noticed that, in addition to medieval fragments, there were particles of tesserae from Roman floors around some rabbit burrows. In making their homes in Littlecote Park the rabbits had brought to light most important evidence of Roman remains.

Turf was removed in June, 1977, for exploratory purposes and it was an exciting moment for Mr. Walters when he found himself looking down at a portion of the Roman mosaic, only twelve inches below the ground surface. The lost mosaic had been found in spite of all the precautions taken by Edward Popham to conceal it in perpetuity.

Mr. Walters and his assistants carefully excavated the site during the summer of 1978, this time with every encouragement from the owner, and the magnificent mosaic was uncovered for the second time. Unfortunately, the roots of the trees so wantonly planted after the 1730 excavation, had caused damage, and the burrowing rabbits, the frost, and the frequent flooding from the nearby river had not improved its condition. Subsidence had also occurred as the mosaic room had originally been constructed over a ditch, a building hazard which the Romans tried to overcome by strengthening the foundations with an extra thick layer of mortar. But in spite of everything, forty per cent of the design depicted in the eighteenth century embroidery had survived.

The damage did not deter Mr. Walters and his team from gathering every minute particle of the mosaic, and a feature of this work was the discovery that the large figure of the central medallion was accompanied by a dog, although the little animal was not shown on the embroidery or engraving of the mosaic. The animal had disappeared in the crack caused by the subsidence, which had evidently occurred before the eighteenth century. Without such a canine companion, the figure would normally be interpreted as being Apollo; but a dog is the traditional companion of Orpheus and so the remarkable rediscovery of the tiny dog led to the crucial identification of the mosaic's central character – Orpheus.

The fact that Orpheus is shown in a standing position is in itself untraditional. He is usually depicted either crouching, or seated on a rock with his lyre resting on his knee. He is surrounded here by four female figures which represent the cycle of life from birth to death. They are standing by animals which are connected in mythology to the god Dionysus. Orpheus faces the western terminal apse, while being flanked on either side by the elaborately decorated north and south apses. To the east there is a rectangular section with four floral panels and four strange sea beasts, two at either end of the pavement.

Dating evidence found beneath the mosaic points to construction around 360 A.D. by which time Orpheus had become the centre of a mystic cult confined to a relatively select group in Roman society. The fact that the Orphic cult of this period was one of the several rivals to Christianity, and that the building which originally housed the mosaic conforms in plan to a typical sixth century church of Byzantium rather than Rome, gives the Littlecote mosaic an important place in any future history relating to the development of Christianity and early Christian architecture.

The mosaic was sent to London for complete and careful restoration. It is now again in its original position although no longer exposed to harmful climatic conditions. It is impossible to describe its beauty – it has to be seen to be fully appreciated.

One mystery still remains – the missing north apse. Although it has been reproduced using modern materials (a fact which is clearly noted) no trace was found of the original section, not even the mortar bedding. The apse was there in 1730 with the other sections – why should that part alone have completely disappeared from the site? Was it taken up and mounted as a trophy? Does it now form part of a decorative panel or floor in an old house in the county or beyond, where its owner is unaware that he houses part of this unique Roman floor?

Perhaps one day it will be found, but in the meantime the excavations continue and the archaeologists have revealed the remains of a medieval village, a first century Roman villa, three hypocausts, and a possible Roman temple. All these have so far come to light in the grounds of a beautiful Tudor manor house – a veritable treasure trove on the banks of the Kennet where the two historic counties of Berkshire and Wiltshire merge to share a precious heritage. Try to go and see it if you can. The excavations are open in the afternoons from Easter to the end of September.

A Man of the Vale

THE Vale of Pewsey inspired a remarkable man who lived amidst its beauty in the early eighteenth century.

When Stephen Duck was born in the tiny village of Charlton St. Peter in 1705 his parents little thought that their son would one day be a recipient of royal patronage. They were poor and could give the boy only a scanty education but as he roamed the Vale he absorbed its every mood and noted everything that went on around him. At the age of fourteen he was apprenticed as a farm labourer, and received the sum of four shillings and sixpence a week.

This meagre wage left little to spare for the books for which the teen-aged boy craved but with a friend who shared the same interests he read anything that came to hand. Together they studied "Paradise Lost" with the help of a dictionary. The "Spectator" and L'Estrange's translation of "Seneca's Morals" were read and re-read until gradually other books, including a volume of Shakespeare, could be procured.

In spite of his poverty Duck married at the age of nineteen but his young wife died in 1730 leaving him with three small children. By this time he was writing poetry and although he burned most of his literary efforts enough of his work was circulated to attract the attention of neighbouring clergy who began to take notice of this local poet. Someone, described as 'a young gentleman from Oxford' asked him to write an epistle in verse, which was afterwards published, but the greatest encouragement came from Mr. Stanley, a clergyman who persuaded the young labourer to write about something he really knew well. "Thresher's Labour" was the result, and this and other country poems brought him to the notice of Queen Caroline, consort to George II. The Queen sent for him and Duck found himself in a strange new world. The hustle and bustle of the London streets and the affectations of the Georgian court must have dazed the simple, village poet, but the Queen was pleased to favour him and not only granted him a pension to alleviate his poverty but helped him to publish his poems.

In 1733 Duck was appointed a Yeoman of the Guard and in the same year he married Sarah Big, the Queen's housekeeper at Kew. His star was ascending rapidly and his lifestyle was now far removed from that of a farm labourer, but more good fortune was to come his way. He was appointed Keeper of the Queen's library at Richmond, a remarkable achievement for a lowly born, self-taught countryman.

Alexander Pope, to whom the Queen sent copies of Duck's early work without revealing his identity, thought little of its quality, but upon learning of the country poet's good character and humble origin, the more celebrated poet became well disposed toward the Queen's protégè, helping him at court and visiting him at Richmond.

Others were not so kindly disposed towards "the phenomenon of Wiltshire" as Duck became known. Swift and Gay were often contemptuous of his poetry and lesser poets were simply jealous of the favour bestowed on him by his royal patroness.

Although disturbed by spiteful criticisms Duck's amazing career continued. He was ordained priest in 1746 and became the preacher at Kew Chapel in August, 1751. The following year he was appointed Rector of Byfleet in Surrey. His clerical duties did not prevent him from writing, and the highly praised "Caesar's Camp on St. George's Hill" was published in 1755.

Unfortunately, in spite of his outstanding success Duck was subject to severe bouts of depression. Perhaps he secretly yearned for a more simple way of life, and the peace and beauty of the Vale which had first inspired his poems.

By the time he was sixty years of age life had become meaningless for him and, tragically, he was found drowned in the River Kennet, behind The Black Lion Inn at Reading, on the 21st March, 1765; a sad end to a fantastic career.

But if his impression on the London scene, and in the realms of English literature was comparatively brief, he is still remembered at Charlton St. Peter. Lord Palmerston donated a field, the rent from which provides for "Duck's Feast", an annual dinner held at The Charlton Cat. Here, in the wayside inn overlooking the village where he was born, a toast is still drunk to the memory of the thresher-poet, Stephen Duck, who proudly trod the streets of London but lost for ever the peace of his native Vale.

Savernake's Royal Bride

THE vast acres of Savernake Forest are now under the care of the Forestry Commission and the public are privileged to be able to wander along the avenues so carefully planned by the noted landscape architect, Lancelot Brown, or 'Capability Brown' as he is better known. He certainly realised the capabilities of Savernake in the eighteenth century when he planned the Grand Avenue and the eight lesser avenues which lead to the centre of the forest. When its owner, the sixth Marquess of Ailesbury, leased the land to the Forestry Commission for a period of 999 years in 1939 he retained the title of Hereditary Warden of Savernake, an honour which had been held by his forbears for over nine hundred years. It twice passed through the female line, in the fifteenth and seventeenth centuries, thus occasioning changes in the names of the holders, but the family links have remained unbroken.

William the Conqueror lost no time in appropriating the forest for his own use when he came to these shores in 1066, and he appointed as the first hereditary warden a man who had served him well at the Battle of Hastings, Richard Esturmy.

Throughout the following centuries the kings of England rode through the forest glades in pursuit of deer which, by the diligence of their successive wardens, were in plentiful supply for the royal sport.

A daughter of the house of Esturmy transferred its privileges and titles to the Seymours when she married into the family in the fifteenth century. A century later, in 1535, it was Sir John Seymour, a friend of King Henry VIII, who was the hereditary warden. He was the father of a large family, six sons and four daughters, and two of his children were already the recipients of royal favour. His son, Edward, was Squire of the Body to the King. His daughter Jane had been lady in waiting to Queen Catherine of Aragon. Now Catherine was divorced and Anne Boleyn was Henry's consort. Lady Jane was at home with her parents at Wolfhall in Savernake when the King signified his intention to hunt in the forest in the early autumn.

This visit was to have far reaching implications for it brought Jane to the close notice of the King. Apparently she had not impressed him during her period at Court but now he was attracted to the small, pale girl of twenty five. She was not an outstanding beauty but perhaps the very contrast between her and Anne Boleyn caught his attention. He was already despondent that the lively Anne had only presented him with a daughter, the Princess Elizabeth, and not the son for whom he longed.

By Christmas Jane Seymour was brought to Court as lady in waiting to Queen Anne. The following year the Queen was in serious trouble, accused of adultery which, for the wife of the King, amounted to a charge of treason. Rumours began circulating that one day Jane would supplant her royal mistress as Queen of England; rumours which had firm foundations. In spite of protestations that she was innocent of the accusations made against her, Anne Boleyn was executed on Tower Green in May, 1536. The King then announced his betrothal to Lady Jane Seymour, and within a few days the marriage was solemnized.

There is a strong local tradition that the marriage took place at Wolfhall although there is no evidence to substantiate the claim.

However, Savernake certainly celebrated the royal wedding. A great barn was hung with tapestries and transformed into a banqueting hall to accommodate all the guests whom Sir John invited to rejoice with him at his daughter's brilliant marriage. The forest resounded to the noise of music and laughter, and the jingling of harness as neighbours rode to join in the merriment.

Alas, the joy was not to last for long. Grief followed in October, 1537, when the Queen died twelve days after the birth of her son, Prince Edward.

Sir John Seymour did not live to see his royal grandson or to know of his daughter's tragic death, for he died in December, 1536. It was therefore Jane's brother, Edward Seymour, now Earl of Hertford, who welcomed the King in 1539 when he returned to Savernake attended by his court. The King arrived on Saturday, August 9th to be greeted by the sound of the medieval hunting horn which is used on such occasions, and stayed until the following Tuesday. During the visit of his royal brother-in-law, the Earl and his household made use of the great barn once again. It was furnished to receive them and Wolfhall itself was placed at the disposal of the King and his courtiers. Lord Hertford's mother and children were housed temporarily at Tottenham Lodge, a small property in the forest.

Poor Jane soon became a memory, but her son inherited the throne on the death of Henry in 1547 and her brother Edward was created Duke of Somerset and Protector of the Realm.

The boy king was persuaded to transfer the ownership of Savernake Forest from the Crown to his uncle and despite the Duke's ultimate disgrace and execution, the family managed to retain the forest which was then handed down through the male line until 1676 when it passed by the marriage of a Seymour heiress to her husband, Lord Bruce, eldest son of the Marquess of Ailesbury.

Both Wolfhall and Tottenham Lodge fell into disrepair and the latter was replaced by the more spacious Tottenham House, but the old barn stood until the nineteenth century. Unfortunately, it became so dilapidated that it was almost entirely demolished around 1875. It was claimed at the time of its demolition that great hooks and nails remained in the oak beams on which the tapestries had been hung for the royal wedding festivities. What a small but touching reminder of the pale Tudor Queen and her delicate son who briefly played their parts in the pages of English history.

St. Aldhelm's Church

BRADFORD on Avon is fortunate in its heritage, both in its natural beauty and its architectural treasures, for this historic town stands on the banks of one of Wiltshire's two River Avons, and numbers amongst its buildings a medieval tithe barn, a parish church which dates from Norman times, and a fine town bridge complete with a little chapel, once used as a prison. But one of its greatest treasures, a pure Saxon church, remained in obscurity for many centuries.

Aldhelm, the great Saxon scholar and first Abbot of Malmesbury, founded a daughter monastery at Bradford on Avon between 672 and 705 A.D., and built a church which he dedicated to St. Laurence. In 1001 King Ethelred presented the monastery, and the Manor of Bradford, to the Abbot of Shaftesbury to provide a safe refuge for the nuns against the insults of the Danish invaders. It was also a suitable hiding place for the remains of his half brother, King Edward the Martyr, who was buried at Shaftesbury after being murdered at Corfe Castle in 979 A.D.

At the beginning of the twelfth century the historian, William of Malmesbury, recorded that the monastery had disappeared, whether by Danish or English action he could not ascertain, but that the little church built by St. Aldhelm was still in existence.

About the time of his writing the growing population of Bradford on Avon, combined with a religious revival which was then taking place, necessitated a larger place of worship and so a parish church dedicated to the Holy Trinity was built and consecrated around 1150 A.D. The small Saxon church now stood neglected and it appears to have been used as a charnel house in the middle ages for it is described as a 'Skull House' on old documents.

Over the centuries other buildings were erected around the outside walls, concealing the identity of the erstwhile church. Eventually a wool factory was built against the west wall and a master's house adjoined the nave which was transformed into a school in 1715. Joists were inserted into the inside walls to carry the floor of an upstairs room where boys were taught the history of England quite unaware that they were in part of their country's heritage. A staircase in the porch gave access to this upper classroom.

Ivy covered the exterior walls in the front of the building and disguised the Saxon architecture, whilst the chancel was converted into a three storied cottage. Fortunately, during alteration work in 1858 two carved angels were discovered built into an interior wall. They were shown to the vicar, Canon Jones, who was interested in archaeology, and he realised that the cottage might be part of an ancient church. This fact was further confirmed when he looked down upon the roof of the building from a terrace of his hillside parish.

Whilst consulting other records in the Bodleian Library, Oxford, the Canon came upon the references made by William of Malmesbury concerning the Church and he felt sure that he had discovered St. Aldhelm's long lost Church of St. Laurence.

As a result of the Canon's concern, the Church was restored to its former beauty but first the school and cottage, as well as the adjoining buildings, had to be bought from their respective owners and all this took time. It was 1871 before the building was vested in Trustees for preservation as an ancient monument.

Professor Edward Freeman examined the Church in 1886 and pronounced it to be "an all but untouched example of a church at the end of the seventh century, or the beginning of the eighth" but more recent examinations have revealed that most of the stonework is of the late Saxon period and it is now thought possible that King Ethelred was responsible for the rebuilding of a later church on Aldhelm's original foundations, thus retaining the size and shape of the earlier Saxon building.

Restoration has been careful and complete. The boarded floor was removed from the chancel to reveal a stone pavement, which is thought to be original, protected most probably by the bones which were carelessly thrown upon it. It would have been felt unnecessary to remove or replace the flooring when the building was being used for such a mundane purpose and when it was used for a cottage the boarded floor covered the cold stones. The staircase and upper floors were removed; stones which had been used to build a chimney were found to belong to the chancel arch and were cleaned and used in its reconstruction. The arch is 9ft 8in high by 3ft 6in wide and is probably the smallest in England.

The nave of the church measures 25ft 2in by 13ft 2in and is 25ft 3in high, while the chancel is 13ft 2in by 10ft and rises to a height of 18ft. The walls in which the Saxon doorways and windows still remain are over two feet thick. An arcading runs entirely round the outside of the building and reded pilasters add to the exterior decoration.

The stone angels have been replaced over the chancel arch where they would have originally been lodged either side of a crucifix, and several large stones found buried near the Church were used to form an altar in 1970. Two possible explanations of their original purpose have been given; they may have been part of the first altar, or they may have come from the shrine of St. Edward the Martyr. But care has been taken to use only those bearing Saxon decoration, so whatever their original function they are of the correct period.

A smaller group above the altar is believed to be part of a Saxon cross – one of seven which were set up to mark the stopping places for the body of St. Aldhelm when it was being transferred from Doulting where he died, to Malmesbury, his place of burial. As one such cross was at Bradford on Avon it seems more than likely that the claim is true, and the insertion of the stones in his Church of St. Laurence is indeed a fitting memorial to the man who first built a place of worship in this beautiful riverside town thirteen hundred years ago.

Acknowledgements

It was sheer delight for my husband and I to travel the highways and byways of Wiltshire in search of these stories and to visit the places of their origin. I would like to thank all who helped us on our way.

Especial thanks must be given to Mrs. Rickard and her friends from the Winterslow Women's Institute, Mrs. Herbert, Mrs. O'Leary and Mr. Caslaw of Purton Stoke, the librarians of Marlborough and Newbury Public Libraries, and to Professor Bryn Walters for information regarding the Orpheus Mosaic at Littlecote Park. Their encouragement has helped to make the writing of these Wiltshire stories particularly enjoyable.